Impact of Digital Technology on Library Collections and Resource Sharing

Impact of Digital Technology on Library Collections and Resource Sharing has been co-published simultaneously as *Journal of Library Administration,* Volume 35, Number 3 2001.

Impact
of Digital Technology
on Library Collections
and Resource Sharing

Sul H. Lee
Editor

Impact of Digital Technology on Library Collections and Resource Sharing has been co-published simultaneously as *Journal of Library Administration*, Volume 35, Number 3 2001.

Routledge
Taylor & Francis Group
New York   London

First published by

The Haworth Information Press®, 10 Alice Street, Binghamton, NY 13904-1580 USA

The Haworth Information Press® is an imprint of The Haworth Press, Inc., 10 Alice Street, Binghamton, NY 13904-1580 USA.

This edition published 2013 by Routledge

Routledge   Routledge
Taylor & Francis Group   Taylor & Francis Group
711 Third Avenue   2 Park Square, Milton Park
New York, NY 10017   Abingdon, Oxon OX14 4RN

Routledge is an imprint of the Taylor & Francis Group, an informa business

Impact of Digital Technology on Library Collections and Resource Sharing has been co-published simultaneously as *Journal of Library Administration*, Volume 35, Number 3 2001.

Cover design by Thomas J. Mayshock Jr.

Library of Congress Cataloging-in-Publication Data

Impact of digital technology on library collections and resource sharing / Sul H. Lee, editor.
    p. cm.
    Papers delivered at a conference held March 1-2, 2001 in Oklahoma City, sponsored by the University of Oklahoma Libraries.
    Co-published simultaneously as Journal of library administration, v. 35, no. 3, 2001.
    Includes bibliographical references and index.
    ISBN 0-7890-1908-6 (alk. paper) – ISBN 0-7890-1909-4 (pbk : alk. paper)
    1. Libraries–Special collections–Electronic information resources–Congresses. 2. Libraries and electronic publishing–Congresses. 3. Academic libraries–Collection development–Congresses. I. Lee, Sul H. II. Journal of library administration.

Z692.C65 I47 2002

2002009618

For Melissa

Impact of Digital Technology on Library Collections and Resource Sharing

CONTENTS

ABOUT THE EDITOR

Sul H. Lee, Dean of the University Libraries, University of Oklahoma, is an internationally recognized leader and consultant in the library administration and management field. Dean Lee is a past member of the Association of Research Libraries Board of Directors, the ARL Office of Management Services Advisory Committee, and the Council for the American Library Association. His works include *The Impact of Rising Costs of Serials and Monographs on Library Services and Programs; Library Material Costs and Access to Information; Budgets for Acquisitions: Strategies for Serials, Monographs, and Electronic Formats; Vendor Evaluation and Acquisition Budgets; The Role and Future of Special Collections in Research Libraries; Declining Acquisitions Budgets;* and *Access, Ownership, and Resource Sharing.* He is Editor of the *Journal of Library Administration.*

Introduction

Sul H. Lee

Since the early 1990s, the expansion of digital collections has been at the forefront of library issues. Many librarians have considered the advent of digital resources as one of the most significant library developments of the twentieth century. Electronic resources have made access to collections easier and, in many instances, eliminated the need to buy costly print sources that are updated or reissued annually. In these areas, digital resources have been considered a money and time saver for libraries.

As with all major changes, however, doubts and negative aspects accompany the positive effects. Recent years have witnessed continuing concerns about the impact of digital collections on academic libraries. What will be the impact of digital books on a library's general collection? How will electronic resources change collection development and how will scholars and students react to digital formats? Will libraries convert to only digital products or will they have to buy both electronic and print formats? Will libraries cease buying print materials in favor of digital resources? Will the traditional concept of libraries as a place of information continue? Will academic libraries retain their central role in the university?

All of these questions are important to librarians, the scholarly community, administrators, and vendors of information products. As each of these groups seeks to accommodate itself within the new digital environment some conflict and indecision is bound to arise. Frequently, answers to the questions asked are equally unsettling and uncertain. There

[Haworth co-indexing entry note]: "Introduction." Lee, Sul H. Co-published simultaneously in *Journal of Library Administration* (The Haworth Information Press, an imprint of The Haworth Press, Inc.) Vol. 35, No. 3, 2001, pp. 1-4; and: *Impact of Digital Technology on Library Collections and Resource Sharing* (ed: Sul H. Lee) The Haworth Information Press, an imprint of The Haworth Press, Inc., 2001, pp. 1-4. Single or multiple copies of this article are available for a fee from The Haworth Document Delivery Service [1-800-HAWORTH, 9:00 a.m. - 5:00 p.m. (EST). E-mail address: getinfo@haworthpressinc.com].

is one thing, though, upon which all groups are beginning to agree. That is that selected digital resources for libraries are highly useful and offer tremendous potential advantage for all groups if utilized in the correct relationships with traditional sources.

Consequently, the 2001 University of Oklahoma Libraries annual conference, held March 1st and 2nd in Oklahoma City, focused upon ways in which libraries might be impacted by digital formats, how they might best use the electronic resources available to them, and how they might overcome some of the difficulties that digital resources present for libraries, information users, and information vendors. The conference brought together nine leading academic librarians and information vendors. Each addressed an aspect of the effect of digital resources on library collections. Their presentations are collected in this volume.

Paula Kaufman, University Librarian at the University of Illinois-Urbana, provided a point of departure by offering twelve predictions about information collections and delivery in research libraries. She acknowledged that digital resources have brought about some radical changes within the library's organizational structure and in the ways libraries provide information and services. Still, she concludes that libraries, as a place, will continue and their central role in the 21st century university will not diminish because of digital resources. Instead, she expects that 21st century library users will have more information available to them and will be better served.

Our traditional concept of the book, however, needs to be rethought or reevaluated according to Clifford Lynch, executive director of ARL's Coalition for Networked Information. Certain types of what we now call books are better suited to the ebook concept than others. These more adaptable types, really databases that used to appear in book format, are becoming increasingly common and libraries are committing to the acquisition of these in an electronic format. The traditional scholarly monograph, however, will evolve with its final digital format still uncertain.

Any discussion of acquiring, preserving, and distributing digital resources should include the vendor's perspective as well. Philip Blackwell, chief executive officer for Blackwell Limited, Oxford, England, one of the western world's leading information vendors in both print and digital formats, offers his views on digital resources in the next chapter. While viewing the trend toward digital books as increasing and inevitable, he notes that librarians, and academic librarians especially, have continued to acquire print materials in record numbers. He concludes that vendors must accommodate the demand for both print and digital mediums to survive in the changing information environment. Conversely, Karen Hunter, a senior vice president for Elsevier Science, has observed that research libraries, increasingly, are choosing electronic journals to the exclusion of print formats. Her informative paper explores some of the reasons and ramifications for these decisions.

Dennis Dillon, assistant director for Collections and Information Resources at the University of Texas-Austin, examines the changing environment that digital resources have brought to librarianship. He is in basic agreement with Clifford Lynch in that he also is not certain what format some of the traditional library media will take. He also concludes that the library will adapt and evolve, but will continue to provide services to scholars and students much as it does today.

President and CEO of the Newberry Library, Chicago, Illinois, Charles Cullen, while optimistic about electronic resources, is wary of wholesale digitization of research collections by libraries. While potentially useful, librarians must be sure that the collections offered in a digital format are accessible to wide audiences and meet standards for long-term preservation and access. While favoring digitization of research collections, Cullen counsels a cautious, cooperative approach to digital conversion of collections by research libraries.

The Texas A & M University Libraries have taken a positive, proactive stance on the changes that electronic resources have brought to the academic library setting according to Dilawar Grewal, Texas A&M's director of the Academy for Advanced Telecommunications and Learning Technologies, and Fred Heath, dean of Texas A & M University Libraries. They posit that academic libraries have a choice as to how they respond to digital resources. Grewal and Heath maintain that there is a tremendous opportunity at hand for libraries to utilize the new information formats and technologies to continue playing a central role as an active partner in the academic research environment. Their contribution to this book explains how Texas A & M developed an electronic information delivery system that allows the University Libraries to be a contributing partner by providing electronic information for research and instruction.

While electronic resources have improved access to many collections, this improvement frequently brings changes in related areas. Digital collections have caused some fundamental changes in the relationship between the ownership of intellectual property and its users. Recent legal trends have favored owners or licensors over users or licensees. This shift has important ramifications for libraries, and Prudence Adler, associate executive director of ARL's Federal Relations &

Information Policy, reviews the key legislation and recent court cases affecting this area of collection building.

The shift to digital resources has brought undreamed of improvements in access to collections, and in keeping selected resources current. At the same time, library administrators face new challenges in providing digital information to students and scholars. The contributors to this volume have offered suggestions for coping with these new challenges and presented observations on what is happening digitally in some of the nation's major research libraries. As electronic resources continue to evolve and their place in academic libraries becomes more familiar and more comfortable, these essays will be looked upon as solutions or forerunners of solutions to many of the concerns that faced librarians in the early years of the 21st century. From that perspective, the essays in this book, indeed, are contributions to the field of librarianship.

Whose Good Old Days Are These?
A Dozen Predictions for the Digital Age

Paula Kaufman

INTRODUCTION

We seem to have an inbred societal tendency to look back to the past as the "good old days." There's the "golden age" of public school education, the golden age of radio, the golden age of television, and just the plain old "good old days." And, in truth, much of the past is worth savoring. But is the past really better than today, or does the view from afar make our memories selective?

At some point in the future, today will be part of the good old days. In order to speculate about what we might savor from the world in which we work today, and what our memories will conveniently forget, we first must have a sense of what tomorrow might be like. Inspired by Brian Hawkins' recent set of ten predictions for technology and higher education,[1] including one that the necessary library infrastructure will be missing as our universities seek success in the emerging distance education marketplace, I offer a set of 12 predictions that characterize how I think the future might unfold. I offer these with the usual caveats that predictions are unreliable at best, that I am no more qualified to make them than anyone else, and that I am not prepared to predict a fixed time at which I think they may actually occur. With my predictions come sets of serious challenges, both to some of the fundamental assumptions we make about academic and research libraries and to the way in which we do our work. Although they center around the theme of this conference,

Paula Kaufman is University Librarian, University of Illinois Library at Urbana-Champaign.

[Haworth co-indexing entry note]: "Whose Good Old Days Are These? A Dozen Predictions for the Digital Age." Kaufman, Paula. Co-published simultaneously in *Journal of Library Administration* (The Haworth Information Press, an imprint of The Haworth Press, Inc.) Vol. 35, No. 3, 2001, pp. 5-19; and: *Impact of Digital Technology on Library Collections and Resource Sharing* (ed: Sul H. Lee) The Haworth Information Press, an imprint of The Haworth Press, Inc., 2001, pp. 5-19. Single or multiple copies of this article are available for a fee from The Haworth Document Delivery Service [1-800-HAWORTH, 9:00 a.m. - 5:00 p.m. (EST). E-mail address: getinfo@haworthpressinc.com].

the impact of the digital age on library collections and cooperation, some of them are much broader in scope and in challenge. After I've offered the entire set, I'll turn back to the question of whether these coming changes will help advance us towards our ultimate dreams and visions of the future or if today, indeed, will be seen rightly as the "good old days."

I share the widely-held dream of having all scholarly and research publications available universally and perpetually on the Internet, along with a set of value-added services that help retain the library's importance to its users and its funders. Although this will not happen fully within the next five to ten years, we will by then be much closer to attaining this vision. While the total transformation of libraries will still await realization, I believe that the academic library's role within the University will remain vital and viable, and probably more important than it is today. That importance will be realized as the library transforms to offer an array of information resources and services not now possible. In addition, the library surely will increase in value as a significant symbol of the "whole," the entirety of the University, especially in the large decentralized research universities that daily seem to grow more and more fragmented.

Here are my predictions, the first of which is not very radical:

1. *Although there will be more distance education offerings, more faculty and students accessing information resources online, and more fully developed and often used online reference services, access to tangible information sources, such as printed books and journals, will still be important.* Until we are able to digitize all of the scholarly resources we now hold in our libraries, or until scholars deem that only digital materials have any value, that is to say until they reject everything not accessible digitally, neither of which will happen, our non-digital materials will continue to have high value to scholars. This means that research libraries will have to continue to operate several systems of access and delivery simultaneously. Clearly, librarians will continue to find ways to make it easier for scholars and students to use those materials not accessible fully via the Internet. For example, if they do not already, the delivery services many libraries now offer will include pickup services–on and off campus–and they will be extended to students and faculty alike. Consortial state-of-the-art storage facilities will allow pruning of duplicatively held items while storage and delivery will become increasingly cost-effective. Librarians will also make it more pleasant and effective for the people who want to use physical materials in the library's physical facilities by reconceptualizing and rede-

signing library spaces to be more comfortable, to accommodate single readers as well as teams of users–one or more of whom may not be physically in the library–and, for those libraries that have not already changed their ways, by permitting, even encouraging, patrons to bring beverages and food with them. Physical facilities, along with virtual ones, will be more accessible to people with various disabilities. On behalf of all users, librarians will have worked hard to lower many barriers to easy access, many of them artificial, that we've imposed all these long decades.

2. *Scholarly communication will continue to reflect the changes of information technology, but not substantially or equally in all of its parts.* In a recent talk entitled "Prophecies,"[2] Willis Regier, director of the University of Illinois Press and current president of the Association of American University Presses, predicted that although publishing on-line is as infinite as imagination, scholarly monograph publishing will remain limited by what always limits publishing: paper. End users will buy more and more paper for their printers, and more and more works will be printed on-demand at copy shops and bookstores. He predicts that as electronic publishing expands, works that are professionally published on paper will be enhanced and printed books will be perceived as having more value. "Many important publishers will publish only on paper and will thrive."[3]

The picture will be quite different in journal publishing, where clearly there will be many changes. We are currently in the midst of the transformation of many important journals into electronic formats and, at least in the disciplines in which currency is critical, electronic journals are greatly preferred and demanded by library users. Current format issues and persistent access problems will likely be solved in the not-too-distant future. We also will likely see the long-vaunted prediction of individual article delivery emerge as the preferred delivery format over the current bundling approach, at least in selected fields. The market for scholarly journals will continue to be dominated by large publishers who offer considerable added value to their products. Pricing models might be more rational and flexible, but prices will continue to rise at rates in excess of general inflation. Simultaneously, though, I think we will continue to see such efforts as SPARC (Scholarly Publishing & Academic Resources Coalition) yield more competition in selected fields. Some of these efforts will succeed in changing market dynamics, pricing, and availability, and some will not, but in the aggregate they will continue to educate both contributors and those who influence buying decisions, and they will slowly transform the ways in which some scholarship is communicated.

Clifford Lynch recently reminded us about the challenges associated with newly emerging genres of digital scholarly communication.[4] Genomic sequences, protein databases, complex multimedia sources, learning objects, and other new forms of information present us with very interesting challenges. Many of these items will appear outside of the traditional systems of scholarly communication, posing problems of how to find, acquire, negotiate, and provide long-term access to them. I think that these challenges will far outstrip the ones we face today, thus leading me to point out at least one area in which today might indeed be seen as "the good old days": the good old days when one could rely primarily on traditional distribution channels, negotiate licenses with a relatively few number of commercial vendors and ensure that the terms of those relatively few contracts were honored.

Many new forms of scholarly communications that are only emerging today will mature in the coming years. Some traditional books are transforming into ebooks, no longer static objects but now dynamic text and text-bearing devices. Within the next few years the various incompatibilities among reading devices should be gone, at least in part, or if not, reading devices will be so inexpensive that they will be offered at little or no cost by publishers and other vendors who want to sell their content.

There are some recent and conflicting predictions about how fast and how large the market for ebooks will grow. John Wicker of Vista Computer Services recently estimated that within 10 years 50% of all published products will be available only electronically,[5] and Malcolm Maclachlan, senior analyst for the research firm IDC, predicted that the U.S. market for digital books, including digital downloads and print-on-demand books, will grow from $9 million in 2000 to $414 million in 2004.[6] Daniel P. O'Brien, senior analyst at Forrester Research, however, predicts slower growth, expecting that sales of ebooks and ebook devices will reach only $251 million in the same period.[7]

But these analysts do predict a rosy future for print-on-demand publishing because, as Maclachlan says, it bridges the gap between traditional and e-publishing by melding the convenience of digital publishing with the familiarity of a paper book.[8] O'Brien, too, sees strong sales of custom-printed trade books, as well as digitized textbooks, ahead. He predicts that digital delivery of custom printed books and textbooks will reach more than $7 billion and will result in a new publishing model that he calls multichannel publishing,[9] in which publishers will manage all of their content from a single, comprehensive storehouse, a repository containing modular book content and structure. If these developments occur as predicted, libraries will be challenged to provide intellectual and content access to digital books, journals, journal articles, new genres, and other materials on an enduring basis.

3. *Our dependence on the MARC format for providing intellectual access to library holdings will continue to diminish.* For decades, librarians have focused much of their energy and resources on providing MARC or MARC-like cataloging records for books, journals, and other traditional formats. In the wake of that effort, however, millions of such "nontraditional" items as special collections, archives, and the like, in which we have invested multi-millions of dollars, have been left virtually inaccessible except by those people who know they exist and where. Staff in these areas have made noble attempts to liberate these holdings for more widespread use by developing finding aids, web-accessible data bases, and other innovative but non-integrative discovery and retrieval tools. For the most part, they have labored in their own dark corners, separate from the groups of experts we engage to provide more traditional cataloging, and often separate from one another, even when several groups might be using similar techniques, such as EAD. Some library staffs, or some parts of them, are now using emerging metadata standards and markup languages for digital materials that integrate more easily with more traditional catalogs, but for the most part, they, too, are laboring in their own corners. And many front-line service librarians are providing a variety of access points and links to a bevy of websites and other information sources. In general, each of these efforts is a separate activity.

We know what our users want. They want to find everything they need in one search, with links from citations to full text, and the resulting documents on their desktops or laptops or palms. But given that the types and genres of such materials are increasing, that not everything will be digital, and thus that their wishes cannot be granted immediately, we at least owe them the chance to discover and retrieve, easily and in as few separate searches as possible, what we own or can provide access to. We know that we will be much better able to do this technologically in the near future and new portal developments point to paths that look exceedingly attractive. How we organize ourselves to accomplish this vision is perhaps less important than the discussions we have and the principles and values we use on which to build our future access systems. However, the organizational issues are not without significance, which leads me to my next prediction.

4. *Technical services as we know it will change, but we might not recognize it or be comfortable with what it is or where it resides within the library.* There are many changes on the horizon that will impact what we now know as "technical services." These include coming changes in distribution methods to accommodate multichannel publishing, similar changes in the distribution of journals as unbundled articles, the need to provide access and intellectual access to new and different kinds of digital materials, the need to provide online intellectual access to the many nontraditional materials we own, the application of emerging metadata harvesting techniques, the emerging new genres of scholarly information, and our desire to provide links and/or portal entries to related appropriate materials (many of which we neither own nor license).

Over the last few decades we have seen and made significant changes to some of the ways in which we perform the various functions that commonly comprise "technical services." We now routinely outsource some of the functions associated with acquiring, cataloging, and making trade publications shelf ready; we apply new methodologies to facilitate discovery and retrieval; and we spend considerable time negotiating and implementing license agreements. Some of our libraries invest significantly in developing standards and best practices to facilitate end-user discovery and use of scholarly information, especially from the "hidden Web"–information such as images, maps, and archival holdings, digitized and held by academic institutions but not accessible through commercial systems or existing Internet search engines–and developing "local resolution" technologies and protocols required to enable efficient and reliable dynamic linking among online information resources, such as from one journal article to another. Is it not interesting that these technical developments more often occur outside the boundaries of our traditional "technical services" than within them, and that often traditional technical services staff are the last to know about and integrate some of these new techniques into their repertoires?

More than two decades ago, my predecessor Hugh Atkinson challenged our thinking about the organization of technical services. His grand thinking–and it was grand in the many senses of that word–mostly did not prove workable in its time and place. But his ideas inspired many important changes in our thinking and practices.

We need to think more grandly again, to think broadly and boldly about what we will have to do to link our users to the scholarly resources we pay for or otherwise make available regardless of format, to facilitate their discovery, retrieval, and use of these items, and to ensure their persistence (the materials, that is; we already know how persistent and impatient our users can be). In addition to the serious intellectual issues this challenge raises, there are some interesting organizational ones. Can we find ways to accomplish our goals without building little bevies of workers each isolated from one another and some very isolated from the ultimate end user? Do we really need to continue to separate the staff who provide this critically important service from the patrons who use it? Taken together, these certainly comprise one of our grandest challenges of the next decade.

5. *Technologies and standards for preserving digital information and assuring perpetual access will soon emerge, but resolution of selection principles and interinstitutional organizational structures in which to ensure a good outcome will develop more slowly.* Preservation programs have developed differently and at different rates in different libraries. Some are comprehensive, well planned, and well implemented. Others are much more hap-hazard.

Lynne Brindley reminds us that we do not have the luxury enjoyed by our predecessors in their curation of printed materials, when they could to a large extent rely on "benign neglect" as a major component of their preservation strategy.[10] Action must be taken from the start to ensure viable and sustainable access to digital content. But this costs money, recurring funds for which external funding agencies cannot be relied, and takes rethinking our traditional ways of organizing both internally and externally to accomplish what we think is most important for the future of the digital era.

We can continue our reliance on declining external support or try to think differently about how to plan and organize ourselves for sustainability. Nicholson Baker's recent article about newspaper preservation[11] raises some important issues we must resolve if we, collectively, are to be successful in preserving our heritage.

Although there is much to dispute about Baker's major points, of which Richard Cox has done a masterful job,[12] Baker raises some grander challenges for librarians: selecting what we are to preserve, determining the best formats, providing intellectual access, and assuring that the preserved items will remain accessible and useable. Clearly, no library working alone can accomplish as desirable an outcome in this area than libraries working together. Among those libraries with missions to gather and preserve important materials, the key issues are who will be responsible for what, who will pay, and where the resources will come from.[13]

6. *Library buildings will be more important in the future.* Although I do not think that Ray Kurzweil's predictions about computers becoming more intelligent than their creators[14] will come true any time soon, and I am not at all sure that society really will want the impersonal environment to which his predictions seem to lead, it seems safe to predict that computers and networks, both wired and wireless, will be nearly ubiquitous in the future. Applications will be almost limitless: personal health monitors connected to local health networks; new types of news displays; intelligent reference guides. As the world of embedded computers expands, many of our activities will receive automatic support from the infrastructure, often without our even being aware of the devices. To rational thinking people this might mean that library buildings will become less important, except to those few souls who need to consult a printed source. On that basis, I am probably not rational, but I think library buildings will take on greater importance in the future.

Jose-Marie Griffiths, in responding to Steve Coffman's ideas about building the "earth's largest library,"[15] agrees, pointing out that exposure to digital resources and services only serves to increase interest in the physical versions.[16] I also think that with users bombarded by information at a pace and quantity we really cannot imagine today, libraries will increasingly become the "safe places" in our society: places safe for intellectual pursuits, for finding information, and for entertainment; places that are safe, or at least safer, from privacy concerns; places that are comfortable to work in, in which one can bring one's desktop but not be tied to it; places in which to interact with other people who use and staff libraries; places to work in groups or teams; places in which help from a real human being is readily available; places in which there is much to be learned; and places that are safe physically. And I suppose I should not overlook the oft-joked about but accurately portrayed use of library spaces to meet and socialize, especially among the undergraduate set. Put another way, I think that our libraries will be ultimate destinations of choice.

It might be easy to dismiss this prediction as a combination of ideological values and wishful thinking, but I hope you'll think about it. My library's annual user surveys show our undergraduates' continued expressed high priority to extend library hours. Members of the University Librarian's Student Advisory Committee and many faculty consistently tell me that they want several of our libraries to be open longer hours, both later in the evening and earlier on weekend days. And student government officers regularly tell the same thing to me, the Senate Library Committee, the Provost, the student newspaper, and anyone else they think can make it happen. Their consistent voice is telling us something important.

7. *There will be fewer library consortia, but they will be larger in size and scope and more powerful than they are today. There will also be many new types of partnerships and collaborative activities that will extend and enhance access for our users.* It is obvious to me that there are now too many library consortia. My institution belongs to so many that it is nearly a full-time job to sort out what products and services each offers at what price and with what conditions. Many of these consortia also require significant amounts of staff time and effort to sustain.

Some state-funded consortia to which we belong provide access to resources for which we pay nothing directly. The benefits are fairly clear, although the true costs of participation are fuzzier. The benefits are also clear, at least from a financial perspective but not necessarily from a service perspective, in our membership in another organization that provides a statewide online integrated library system. Although some consortia bring our users or our universities significant benefits, the panoply of organizations, and the time and energy we spend in all of them collectively, is a mini-nightmare. In the state of Illinois the consortial resource purchasing scene has become so cluttered that our innovative Director of the State Library, Jean Wilkins, has created an organization to keep on top of all their offerings. How long can this go on?

Actually, I think the more interesting "action," especially in terms of making more resources more available and providing the necessary supporting services, will come through new types of collaborations and partnerships. Libraries will not be effective by working alone or only with other libraries. Bill Regier predicts that the most successful digital projects will be those that involve collaboration. Collaboration, he says, "improves ambition and critique and adds the pleasures and comfort of friendship . . . Collaborations of genius, not genius alone, will create the most impressive projects."[17] Bill, I am glad to say, puts his money where his mouth is. His organization and mine, along with, hopefully, the Newberry Library (with whom the UIUC Library has purchased two medieval manuscripts jointly in another example of a different kind of collaborative effort) are in the planning stages of a very interesting project that will produce and distribute digital products of rare and unique materials.

I think it is also clear that consortia that only extend horizontally are not poised well for success. Analyses of e-businesses that have failed recently show that, in part, their lack of success can be attributed to their failure to extend their businesses vertically. If we think those analyses have some relevance to libraries, and I, for one, do, then we must think about vertical partnerships and collaborations. I'm glad to say that many libraries are already moving in this direction. Some examples include Stanford's new Dark Cave initiative in which it is hoping to partner with many content producers and providers to test a huge digital repository model, and the Columbia University programs that involve the library, information technology organizations, scholars, and the university press in developing new ways to deliver content digitally, along with measures of their success. Many libraries, mine included, work with museums and the K-12 community to extend the reach of our collections to other constituencies while extending some of theirs to ours. Health Science librarians have long provided us with an interesting model in which some medical librarians become part of the teams of health service providers who work directly with patients. The model's lack of adoption by the rest of the library community has always puzzled me. I suppose it is viewed by some people as too resource-intensive.

Although nothing I have just said precludes consortia, partnerships, and collaborations that cross national boundaries, I would be remiss if I did not point out the increasingly global perspectives, arrangements, and organizations that will be key to libraries' success in the digital age. The Mortenson Center at the University of Illinois at Urbana-Champaign, along with other international efforts, surely will serve as inspirational models for the future.

8. *Services in the age of the never satisfied library user will be influenced by the continuing commercialization and development of the Internet and the Internet will be influenced by libraries.* We know that the Web is far from complete. Tim Berners-Lee, inventor of the Web, reminds us that the web is only half-finished. The second half of the information revolution, which he terms "the Semantic Web," will be characterized by databases that grow smarter and work together to solve problems.[18] But it still will not produce the totality of information that our users need and it will not provide access to what it does have easily, reliably, and in a way that separates the virtual wheat from the chaff. Although I already have raised implicitly the question "what good is a grand collection of scholarly information if users can't find and use it?" it bears raising again in the context of the set of supporting services libraries will be expected to provide.

As we move closer to my dream of universal access in perpetuity, I must add yet another, one that former colleagues of mine know has been one of my dreams for many years now: user self-sufficiency. The goal is to have satisfied library users who can find and use appropriate and reliable resources themselves. This means that libraries must offer web sites that compete, at least in principle, with commercial sites. In some respects I suppose I aspire for the library to be a "killer app."

Steve Coffman has been much influenced by Amazon.com.[19] Although Amazon.com is a bookstore, and not a library, it offers services that are reworked versions of some of our more primitive ones. Following Amazon's lead, libraries soon will be using sophisticated systems that will help keep users current, that will take them to e-preprints and other works in progress, that will help them find what we now consider non-mainstream and grey literature, and that will allow them to personalize their own library access pages. Highly sophisticated and effective portals will serve, in part, as the basis for some of these new services. At this point, however, I will not predict libraries' role in developing these portals, except for the obvious prediction that they will develop them in fields for which there is no commercial market for them.

At present, reference librarians are working hard to test new ways to provide real-time online reference services, services that will enable users and librarians to look at and work with the same online sources simultaneously. Some of these efforts are being undertaken alone, others are inter-institutional collaborative efforts. We know that email reference has not been terribly successful and we can guess some of the reasons. And we know that Ask Jeeves® type services are ineffective, although our users do not always know it. Now that we have more sophisticated software and real-time capability we have an opportunity to think differently about how we offer reference services. And we have an opportunity to think differently both about what we mean by reference, who we need to provide it (i.e., what sets of talents, knowledge, and skills), and how we organize to deliver it. We will also have to confront yet another area in which we could offer a service simultaneously in different formats. It is yet another opportunity to think grandly about the future, or not to think about it at all, letting it evolve as time progresses.

If we believe Ray Kurzweil's predictions that people will be interacting more with virtual humans than real humans, we will have thousands of virtual Marians sitting on our networks ready and presumably able to provide a panoply of reference services. I do not think we will. Knowing that not all sources will be accessible for many years to come, I still take heart in Jose-Marie Griffiths' predictions and I still believe that our faculty and students will want some reference and other services face-to-face or, if they cannot visit our facilities physically, voice-to-voice. It will take many years before in-depth reference consultations can be carried out differently and, as we develop them, we can well influence the services offered by the commercial sector.

9. *Although libraries will face increasing competition from the commercial sector, a series of shakeouts there will "showcase" libraries' stability as a valuable asset.* The current decline in the technology sector is probably an aberration in what will be the normalization of the marketplace. Last year's shakeout was a phenomenon created by a number of factors whose confluence might not happen again for many years. The booming economy created vast sums of venture capital, much of which poured into start-up tech companies whose promise was not so much sustained growth and profitability, but rather attraction to a public eager to make huge investment gains in short periods of time. I predict that in the future technology firms will grow, and fail, in ways to which traditional firms are more accustomed.

At present, there are a number of companies entering what has been traditionally part of the market dominated by libraries and library service. We do not yet know what they will vie for, but whatever it is it will not devalue libraries overall. We have never been able to offer everything our users want, and even when my dream materializes, we will not necessarily be able to make it all available. Libraries, however, will continue to be the point of entry to the information universe for many of its users. I think that large libraries will continue to have special value and will continue to provide their universities a competitive edge. However, we also will have to know how to measure and assess what we deliver; that is, we have to know how well we meet our users' expectations and needs, and we must have a better handle on the costs and effectiveness of what we are doing. And even though there are many interesting but incomplete efforts underway, we really do not know how to do that now. I think we will continue to see increased activity in this area that is critical to our future success.

I firmly believe that the library "brand" will increase in value over time. Librarians add credibility and validation to the collections they build, and this validation is becoming increasingly important in cyberspace, where anyone can publish anything. Although search engines can help find some things on the web, they cannot provide the objective validation that librarians can. Librarians are just about the only people who can link cyber-resources and collections to physical resources and collections.[20] And that is our competitive edge.

10. *Public policy issues will have more impact on libraries' success than technology issues.* This is not a hard prediction to make. For several years now, with the passage of the Digital Millenium Copyright and

Sonny Bono Copyright Extension Acts, the introduction of the anti-database bills, and introduction of filtering legislation on the federal and state level, and now attempts to enact UCITA in the states as well as actions attempted by the World Intellectual Property Organization, it is increasingly clear that such public information policies both here and abroad have had and will continue to have profound impacts on what and how libraries provide access to scholarly information resources. We will continue to see such issues as intellectual property laws, filtering, privacy, confidentiality, security, and liability have much greater impact than ever before. With changes in the federal administration and soon the Supreme Court, it is impossible to underestimate the serious nature of these and other related issues. Librarians individually, collectively, and through our national and international organizations, in coordination with our universities, must be alert and diligent to them, picking the most important battles because neither we nor our institutions are likely to have sufficient financial resources, and perhaps even energy, to battle successfully on every front.

11. *The supply of librarians to work in academic libraries will continue to dwindle and this will create a serious barrier to future success.* The current spate of retirements among academic librarians will continue throughout this decade, as the librarians who entered the profession in the 1960s, 70s, and early 80s near traditional retirement age or take advantage of omni-present early retirement offers. In the past, replacements for these retirees were not hard to attract. Experienced librarians appeared to be much more mobile than they seem to be today, and there was an adequate supply of new graduates eager to work in academic libraries.

But today, and of more long-term consequence, are the changes in library education. The closure of many private library schools in the 1970s and 1980s has not been compensated by expansion in output by the remaining schools. The number of graduates has fallen from about 8000 in the mid-1970s to about 5000 in 1996/97.[21] In addition, library education is changing from traditional library offerings to information science and technology.[22] We are seeing lower percentages of new graduates going into traditional library settings, of which the academic library is just one.

So, if there are fewer trained professionals, and increasing demands for library resources and services, how are we to manage? Again, it is time to think grandly about the future. We must find strategies to continue to attract highly talented people to our doors, train and develop them, mentor them, nurture them. Although this cry has been heard before, it is time for new thinking: time to develop new partnerships with schools of library and information science, time to develop new ways to find and mentor people with the skills and talents we need; time to rethink our requirements for initial and continuing employment. How can we find the flexible people we want if we are not flexible and nimble in our thinking about them?

Finally, my last prediction. It is one that turns Brian Hawkins' prediction that the necessary library infrastructure will be missing on its side (if not its head).

12. *The necessary university infrastructure will be missing.* Even as we seek to provide for our faculty and students access to additional information in new ways and in new formats, the usefulness of these acquisitions is limited by the state of the art in information technology and an inability to fully integrate our array of digital information resources. Standards and protocols for authentication and authorization will not be available on most university campuses for several years; neither will sufficient fidelity to support class-specific electronic reserves in a uniform and seamless manner. Available technologies and protocols for routinely and reliably linking between online catalogs, related bibliographic databases, and the full-content of scholarly publications are simply insufficient. It is critical that work underway to address these and similar problems be continued and accelerated.[23]

CONCLUSION

Are today's times the good old days? I suppose that when we look back on them these times will seem relatively simple. Fewer choices, less ambiguity, fewer license agreements, less complicated public policy issues, and probably more financial resources. More importantly, however, our users today will seem much less better served. Tomorrow our resources and services will extend and reach much farther, and we will be working in global partnership with new groups in exciting and productive new ways. If we are still fixated on the past–on today–as perfect, we will continue to fool ourselves about the past just as we fool ourselves today. I, for one, do not want to look back, except to learn from history. What's ahead is the chance to think differently and grandly about the future, the chance to see more of our dreams realized, and it is that future to which I invite you to join me.

NOTES

1. Brian L. Hawkins, 2000. "Technology, Higher Education, and a Very Foggy Crystal Ball." *EDUCAUSE Review* 35 (6): 64-73.

2. Willis Regier, October 2000, "Prophecies" (presentation at The Impact of Electronic Publishing on Scholarly Communication: A Forum on the Future, University of Illinois at Urbana-Champaign Library). Available from the author.

3. *Ibid.*

4. Clifford Lynch, October 2000, "Untitled" (presentation at The Impact of Electronic Publishing on Scholarly Communication: A Forum on the Future, University of Illinois at Urbana-Champaign Library). Contact the author for information.

5. Paul Hilts, January 1, 2001, "Ready for the Revolution," *Publishers Weekly* 248 (1): 58.

6. Lori Enos, December 20, 2000, "Report: E-Book Industry Set to Explode," *E-Commerce Times* <www.ecommercetimes.com/perl/story/6215/html>. [Accessed January 9, 2001] A copy of this article is available.

7. "eBooks Will Flop, But Print-On-Demand and Digital Textbooks Will Thrive, Predicts Forrester Research." Forrester Press Releases, December 22, 2000. <www.forrester.com/ER/Press/Release/0,1769,470,FF.html> [Accessed January 9, 2001] A copy of this press release is available.

8. Enos, *op. cit.*

9. Forrester Press Release, *op. cit.*

10. Lynne Brindley, 2000, "Preservation 2000: Keynote Speech." (Presentation at Preservation 2000: an international conference on the preservation and long term accessibility of digital materials, December 8, 2000.) <http://www.bl.uk/concord/otherpubs_speeches04.html>.

11. Nicholson Baker, 2000, "Deadline: A Desperate Bid to Stop the Trashing of America's Historic Newspapers," *The New Yorker*, July 24, 2000, pp. 42-61.

12. Richard J. Cox, "The Great Newspaper Caper: Backlash in the Digital Age," *FirstMonday*, <http://firstmonday.org/issues/issue5_12/cox/> [Accessed January 11, 2001] A copy of this article is available.

13. Battin, Patricia et al. *Assuring Library Resources for the New Millenium*, p. 12. No place or date provided. Available from the author.

14. Ray Kurzweil, 1999, *The Age of Spiritual Machines: When Computers Exceed Human Intelligence* (New York, New York: Viking), p. 279-280.

15. Steve Coffman, March 1999, "Building Earth's Largest Library: Driving Into the Future," *Searcher* 7 (3): 34-46.

16. Jose-Marie Griffiths, August 2000, "Deconstructing Earth's Largest Library," *Library Journal* 125 (13): 44-47.

17. Regier, *op. cit.*

18. "The Web Turns 10," January 1, 2001, *The News-Gazette* (Champaign, IL), p. D1-D2.

19. Coffman, *op. cit.*

20. Griffiths, *op. cit.*

21. U.S. Department of Education, 2000, *Digest of Educational Statistics*, Table 247.

22. Andrew R. Albanese, Norman Oder, Michael Rogers, and Evan St. Lifer, December 2000, "How the Year's Top Stories Will Impact You . . . in 2001," *Library Journal* 125 (20), p. 74-76.

23. Tim Cole, 29 December 2000, *Possible Updates for Barriers/Opportunities.* [Internet, e-mail to the author]. A copy of this is in the author's possession and may be consulted by contacting the author at <ptk@uiuc.edu>.

What Do Digital Books Mean for Libraries?

Clifford Lynch

The topics I want to address revolve around digital books, e-books, and this whole complex of issues. I will warn you right up front, this is not a tidy subject. There are a lot of different issues converging here. And there is a tremendous amount of confusion that is being generated. I am going to try and talk at least to some extent about issues as they relate to libraries, but I think we need to recognize that fundamentally these issues are about communication; they are about authors, and readers, and how authors communicate with readers. And just as libraries have always been the facilitators of access to that record of communication and the stewards of that communication, they inevitably, through the debates around what happens to the book in a digital world, will get dragged into this in numerous different ways.

We also need to recognize that there is another funny dichotomy at work here. That's the dichotomy between things that are being produced mainly for the scholarly market and things that are being produced mainly for the consumer market. We tend to think and talk a lot about material that is produced for the scholarly market and, certainly, if we look at where the budgets of academic and research libraries go, they do go predominately to scholarly journals and scholarly monographs and things of that nature.

In fact, academic libraries also collect things out of the consumer market. The partition, the wall between consumer and scholarly mate-

Clifford Lynch is Executive Director, Coalition for Networked Information, Association of Research Libraries.

The author is grateful to Dean Sul H. Lee for transcribing the talk.

This is a lightly edited transcript of a talk given from notes, and it retains the informal tone of the talk.

[Haworth co-indexing entry note]: "What Do Digital Books Mean for Libraries?" Lynch, Clifford. Co-published simultaneously in *Journal of Library Administration* (The Haworth Information Press, an imprint of The Haworth Press, Inc.) Vol. 35, No. 3, 2001, pp. 21-32; and: *Impact of Digital Technology on Library Collections and Resource Sharing* (ed: Sul H. Lee) The Haworth Information Press, an imprint of The Haworth Press, Inc., 2001, pp. 21-32. Single or multiple copies of this article are available for a fee from The Haworth Document Delivery Service [1-800-HAWORTH, 9:00 a.m. - 5:00 p.m. (EST). E-mail address: getinfo@haworthpressinc.com].

21

rial, is not clear at all. It is a very porous wall and one of the things that we are reminded of, again and again, is that this is a wall that moves over time.

Today's popular culture is the raw material of tomorrow's scholarship and it is very interesting to look at what has happened to research libraries over the last 20 years with various genres of print materials that they scorned back in the 30s, 40s and 50s. Some have now become hot items for scholarly inquiry and they have had to go out, off and on, to the collectors market or to rely on donations, to gain stewardship of this material to support the new generation of scholars. So we need to recognize that this is a complex world out here, and that academic libraries need to be concerned with what is happening in the consumer marketplace as well as the scholarly marketplace.

I think there are two things going on. One is that we are seeing the inevitable progression of certain genres of books into the digital world. And I will talk quite a bit about that progression and some of the ramifications of it. The other thing we are seeing, which is a very complicated and confusing factor, is an enormous marketplace and public relations hype around something that has come to be called, for want of a better term, e-books. In fact what we are seeing is a very careful marketing campaign to start positioning these as the future of the book in the digital world. I believe that the way that is being positioned right now is both very narrowly construed, very limiting and also very troublesome for a lot of reasons I'll go into.

Some of this is being driven as well, by the fact that we have very different traditions when we look at the book moving toward the digital world and, let's say, music becoming more digital, and I will underscore that term "more digital." For a very long time we have dealt with recorded music through mediating technology. You need a lot of apparatus to make an LP turn into sound; you need even more sophisticated apparatus to make a CD turn into sound. Books, in contrast, are very hearty sorts of things. They don't need a lot of mediating apparatus. Once you have a book the human visual system handles the mediation. So, what we have seen in music is this kind of incremental progression from analog recording on LPs to digital encoding on audio CDs, and now we are starting to see issues about music taking on a more disembodied existence on the network, in part, through an enormously ironic sequence of events.

The audio CD started life as a consumer product–remember it really did, there was the audio CD, played on audio CD players, which were consumer electronic devices. And then there were these weird things called CD ROMs which belonged over in the computer industry. And what happened is magnetic disks got bigger and cheaper, and CD ROM readers got cheap and proliferated as computer peripherals–and because of format compatibility these CD ROM readers could also read audio CDs. Suddenly music became subject to the kind of manipulations that characterize digital information in a computational rather than consumer electronics environment, and of course, computers were networked and, all of a sudden, this consumer product started turning into a free flowing kind of digital object. Consider Napster, for example, a completely unpredictable surprise from the perspective of people inventing new audio CD technology 20 years ago and one that is giving rise to a lot of rather draconian reaction that is being pursued by the music industry. I would invite you to investigate a thing called the Secure Digital Music Initiative (SDMI), for example, which basically envisions the next generation of music as kind of locked up in a very controlled way as it moves around so that it can't get loose for free and uncontrolled redistribution and replication.

Now the jump with consumer books entering the digital world is a very large one. There has been no kind of intermediate creeping through mediation, through phonograph records and audio CDs in any significant way. The jump is really from the printed hard copy physical artifact book all the way into the digital world, and that is a jump that many people are nervous about and has a lot of unexpected ramifications, which I will explore in a minute. Let me start by painting a kind of broad picture around digital books before we look at what's going on with the e-book movement.

I think the first thing we need to recognize is that when we talk about books many different things come to mind: novels, monographs, dictionaries, to give just a few examples. There is in fact an enormous variety of stuff that is published between two covers and that we honor with the notion of "book" as an important cultural artifact, as an important means of communication. Some of these things really never fit between covers very well at all. In fact, I would argue that the first digital books were databases that were sort of brutalized into printed form because we didn't have the technology to affordably make them into databases that people could use. Think about abstracting and indexing information. Once upon a time there were books called *Index Medicus*. This is not a hot seller anymore.

Even more compelling perhaps, some of you may be old enough to remember the joyous process of attempting to use the printed *Science Citation Index*. This is clearly something that in a good world never should have been a book. It really should have been a database, which it has become. In fact, we are seeing all of the genres that were slammed between those two covers evolving towards the digital world at different rates and finding different destinies.

Encyclopedias ... once upon a time homes, families, bought the *Encyclopedia Britannica,* this great long expensive run of books. I gather that this is not selling especially well anymore and that those people who went around door to door or showed up in the grocery store trying to sell you print encyclopedias one volume at a time have gone on to other things at this point. Encyclopedias again are something where they really work better in digital form. Think about their characteristics. You want to be able to search, there's lots of linking between material, it's very valuable to be able to incrementally update, it's nice to be able to include a generous amount of multi media which can, if you do it in print, if you include lots of photographic plates, really run up the cost of the printed work but is much easier to do lavishly in digital form. All of these things make encyclopedias much more natural inhabitants of the digital world.

In fact, we are seeing not just things that were historically in encyclopedias moving to the digital world but, I would almost argue that we are seeing a real emergence of the tradition of encyclopedia building in the digital environment embodied in a particular genre of web site. We are seeing lots of people building specialized websites that are very similar in spirit to specialized print encyclopedias. Images of, and textual descriptions of the flora or fauna of specific regions, exotic skin diseases, specialized art or architecture kinds of things, encyclopedias on how to raise and treat various kinds of animals, an enormous range of these things. When you visit these websites you are seeing, in some sense, a kind of intellectual descendant of the encyclopedia genre. It has many of the same characteristics. You read it in small pieces. It's incrementally updated.

We are seeing lots of things turning into digital books.

I want to make a careful distinction here between digital books and printed books that are stored in digital format. There is a lot of that going on as well. And I will argue that the distinction is that digital books make explicit use of the capabilities of the digital environment. Digitalized print books typically are simply things that are produced by the process of imaging printed books, or, perhaps rather than imaging, taking PDF files that were generated in course of the publication cycle that led to the print book, or maybe even HTML markup that was generated somewhere along the line.

The fundamental issue at least to me is there has been no rethinking here. The author's intent, the genre practices, are basically about communicating on paper and, not at all surprisingly, when many readers encounter these kinds of books, just like when they encounter journal articles which are, in many cases, still designed for print but shipped around and stored in digital form, they do the obvious thing. They do a little looking around until they find the parts they want to read and then they print those parts on paper for reading. The content is designed for a paper user interface it works well on a paper user interface. It may make sense to store it digitally and move it around digitally but fundamentally the use environment is print. Those things I don't think of as digital books. I think of those things as ways that we are using the capability of the digital environment to make moving around and storing and providing access to paper books more convenient, and I think of it as having a big print on demand factor for successful deployment and user acceptance.

But to return to digital books. I've already indicated that digital books have largely eliminated some print predecessors like abstracting and indexing tools and encyclopedias.

But here are some other things that come between two covers that have been much slower to move into true digital books. One of them is the scholarly monograph. Some of the most fascinating thinking that I believe is going on right now is, what do you do with the scholarly monograph when you rethink it for the digital world? I'd invite you to look at some of the writing that people like Robert Darton have done, to look at some of the work that is coming out of the Mellon Foundation funded collaborations involving the American Council on Learning Societies and the American Historical Association. Here we have scholars who have written print books and who are now intrigued by the digital environment, who are looking at what can you do to make a monograph a more effective tool for documenting and communicating scholarship by exploiting the digital environment. And it's very early days here yet. It's not clear what's going to work and what isn't. This is an experimental environment right now. I would speculate that we are going to find that some types of scholarly argument, in fact, have a very linear quality and probably are going to be happier for the foreseeable future in paper. The destiny of all genres of printed books is not digital, other than as a storage and shipping around medium, I would argue.

Similarly we have the textbook. There is a lot of very interesting experimentation going on in how can we rethink textbooks for the digital world. This is leading us down fascinating paths that start raising questions about connections with instructional technology, connections with the use of technology in the classroom, how much these things turn into active learning objects. Again, a very open field of inquiry.

Finally, there is the novel. Those novels that people trot out and club you with whenever you talk about digital books and say, "Digital books will never happen because I like to read novels in the bathtub and on the beach." Novels really don't seem to work very well as digital works, or at least I haven't seen any that are persuasive. They don't seem to be able to take advantage of the opportunities of the digital medium, but they suffer all of its drawbacks because they are about extended linear reading. It may be that someone is going to construct some compelling new forms of storytelling for the digital media. I think that is likely, but they may be something very different than the tradition of the written word novel that typically makes little or no use of illustration or other kinds of multimedia. It may be that as we look to storytelling in the digital environment, the genre antecedents may be found elsewhere; maybe they are movies, maybe they are comic books (graphic novels), but they probably aren't the written novel as we have practiced it for the last hundreds and hundreds of years. I have a feeling that novels are going to resist transition to digital books. But I do think that as we look at the frontiers of scholarship there is a lot of very exciting, interesting stuff going on in the world of digital books.

I want to just say parenthetically, without spending time on it today, that there is also some promising work going on in the digitalization of older books. It's clear that doing that makes them more accessible, often provides them with wider use. It provides searching, it brings back material that is sort of lost from people's intellectual radar screens. We've seen this already with journals–the extensive retrospective programs that are being carried out by JSTOR and by some scientific and scholarly socieities, for example, are making the older journal literature much more accessible. So that's an important set of developments but it's about something else than the sort of rejuvenation of authorship in the digital media I've been discussing. I would say that this digitalization of older books is going to be a critical area for libraries to track and to think about strategically because of the impact on access. But this is another set of issues for another time.

Having set the scene concerning digital books let me say a few words about ebooks. Ebooks are very weird things. You have all seen ebooks. It is impossible to have missed them. These little things are being marketed as the digital substitute for the hard cover book, and, in fact, their marketplace has changed radically.

Two years ago, this was a marketplace of start-ups, Neuvo Media, who sold the RocketBook, Softbook, GlassBook, and many others (not all of which made it to the stage where they shipped products). Now it is fundamentally a market place with three giants in it. You may not realize this. All the little folks, all the start-ups have been bought up. There is Adobe, which bought Glassbook. There is Microsoft which markets the modestly named Microsoft Reader and there is a company that you have probably never heard of called Gemstar, which happens to own a few other small things like *TV Guide* and went on an acquistions binge, buying up several ebook start ups about a year and a half ago.

Those are the players. And really only one of them, Gemstar, is still building these book appliances. Adobe and Microsoft are both building software book readers that live on personal computers. There is also an assortment of players that come out of the personal digital assistant industry, the PalmPilot for example, who are taking on a role as delivery platforms for ebooks.

Whether appliances, software readers, or PDAs, ebooks are being presented in a very strange way. They are being presented as literal substitutes for hard copy books. Indeed, so literal, that some of them have buttons you can push or click that turn the pages. How phenomenally silly to think of such a literal translation into the digital environment. And I can assure you that these ebooks, at least today, are not doing a lot of integration of interactive models and databases, and the broad dynamic world of networked information, all of those exciting capabilities that we think about when we consider how we might reinvent the scholarly monograph in a very rich digital environment.

I want to highlight a few other things I find peculiar in the way that ebooks are being promoted. I've told you about the substitutability sort of notion, this "Throw your printed book away and get an ebook reader and when you tire of the book you have you can pour a new book into it." That in fact is not what is going on. If you look at what people seem to be reading on a lot of these devices, often it is not monographs at all because a lot of people find reading monographs on-screen very tiresome. It is much more ephemeral stuff–magazines, newspapers, material of that sort. Short articles, selected by the user from bulky printed collections of these short articles. And if you look at the economics around that kind of material it is very different and quite a bit more compelling for the publishers and perhaps for the readers than traditional consumer books.

When you consider a book, the physical cost of producing a book is a very small part of its price. Most of the money is in the distribution, wholesale, retail chain, and all of that. Ebooks cut out some of that depending on the business models you choose to believe. But the question is, who's going to get that newly available money? Are they going to drop prices, make bigger profits, or pay authors better? Things like newspapers and magazines live on a much slimmer margin where they are producing all this paper that gets recycled every day. You have a big day-in, day-out delivery problem. These are products where the economics of moving this ephemeral stuff electronically, and looking at it electronically, and discarding it electronically when you are done with it, is very attractive financially for everybody, as well as often convenient to the reader. So, I would be very cautious about thinking that the main thing people will be reading on these reading devices is books, at least in the near future.

Second point, and this is very important and is going to lead into my third and last point about these sort of portable book readers. This notion of substitution is already a considerable falsehood. The existing appliance book readers don't hold a single book, they hold 10 books. Maybe a little more. The software book readers hold as many books as you are willing to buy disk space for. What you are really starting to see here is technology that is going to lead to portable libraries.

A portable personal library is a very different beast than a portable ebook. And it comes with very different cultural baggage. It comes with very different marketing considerations. It comes with very different pricing structures. Let me just invite you to think about a couple of things. If you're buying individual books, you make individual choices. If you are going to go out and buy a library, most people are not going to hand pick it. They may hand pick a few things around the margin, but they are going to go to a library supplier.

Just think about what is happening in the music industry. If you look at some of the rhetoric that is coming out of the large music companies about what they would like to see in a commercial post-Napster world, they speak about music as a service. You subscribe to music, write large, for a few dollars a month and you get to play all the music you want out of this sort of music collection that comes from someplace. This could have some very interesting ramifications for libraries. It could have some very interesting ramifications for readers. For the whole marketing chain, it's something that bears some very careful thinking about.

My last set of points about ebooks will take me back to libraries for some concluding remarks. There are some other ways, important ways, in which ebooks are really different from the printed books they were designed to emulate. You typically can't print it, you can't annotate it and print your annotations. Whether implemented in a closed consumer electronics appliance or in software on a general purpose computer, ebooks are designed to live in a technology environment that protects and controls the content. They just choose not to implement a variety of features that consumers might find attractive, and the software and hardware developers say "if we put in those sort of features the publishers won't publish and provide content in digital form" and the publishers say "we are concerned about the uncontrolled spread of this material, just look at the poor music industry, and we must have technical mechanisms to protect our properties" and so we will only produce and market books in digital form under these very tight controls. You can't give an ebook away, you can't swap it to a used bookstore for a credit for something else you might like. Most of these things don't seem to be on the program right now. Sure, you can loan your ebook reader to a friend but, when that is a personal library next year, how many friends do you feel good enough about to let walk off with your whole personal library and how long can you afford to be without it? Interesting questions. And of course it's anyone's guess whether these kinds of controls will ultimately be acceptable in the consumer marketplace. The early evidence is that they may not be, but it's hard to tell how much of the problem is just awkward, user-unfriendly implementation and how much is real, deep, consumer resistance to the constraints being imposed.

There are many other things that we don't understand about ebooks and how the market for these is likely to evolve. For the first time, if ebooks take off, we'll see the real introduction of cycles of technical progress, and technical obsolescence, into the publishing industry. We've seen these things play out in music. People who had LPs went and bought the same music over again when audio CDs came up. Most consumers didn't expect to be able to trade in their LP and get a CD for maybe a buck extra or something (and certainly the industry didn't make them such an offer). Instead they just bought it all again, in fact the way things work some people have bought the same music three or four or five times by now, in different formats and different packaging, hopefully with some incremental improvements in quality or comprehensiveness (like bonus tracks) in each new version. From the industry point of view, this is an evergreen product; the music industry made a ton of money on the transition from LPs to CDs.

We have very different expectations about books. We have expectations that if we want them to, books and printed matter last a lifetime. We have expectations that parents who have books that they enjoyed as children can stash them away and share them with their children and their grandchildren. I wouldn't want to bet that formats are going to stay stable in the emerging ebook industry so that the ebook that I bought in

2001 still works in 2040. I would expect that I will probably have to acquire the content a few more times or maybe the publisher will give me an upgrade plan. We don't know.

This whole notion of obsolescence, which is actually going to be I think a big deal in the consumer world because of very strongly held assumptions about the way printed material (or electronic materials emulating print) should behave, has yet to be challenged in the marketplace. Now, I don't want to suggest that what is happening with ebooks in the consumer marketplace is an entirely evil thing that is simply steamrolling the consumer. Just think about this one scenario, which is really fascinating: some of the publishers are saying "Well, we will keep a record of what ebooks you have bought. If you lose your ebook reader, if somebody steals it, if you buy a new one, you can get the books back." What a tremendous idea. No more having people lose their library to a natural disaster or something like that. I'm not sure how you are going to split up a digital library in a divorce, that's a different matter. And yes, there are some troublesome privacy issues to be considered. But, all of a sudden there you have a much greater persistence in the face of certain kinds of problems than what consumers have been used to, and this is real new value to the consumer.

This is just one example. There is a whole set of rights–and it is not just rights in the legal sense, it is also sort of marketplace norms, commonly accepted terms and conditions and expectations–about content that are under renegotiation around ebooks. Some of them are explicit and some of them are implicit, but I think they are going to be a crucial factor in the consumer market place.

Now let me return to libraries for my final couple of points. There is a real problem with consumer ebooks right now in the library world. Since they really aren't designed to be lent and since the helpful people who are building the software, hardware, digital rights management, and media packaging are not very keen on lending these things, there is a very real danger that libraries are simply going to be cut out of the loop. If the material can't be circulated the only way that libraries would be able to acquire it is fundamentally under the same kind of terms that are available to the consumer. In other words, they could literally buy ebook readers and put a couple of books on them and circulate the ebook readers. A few libraries are doing that today, at least on an experimental basis, and with the sort of limited success that you might expect, given that they are trying to repurpose a system designed to do something else. Or, alternatively, libraries can try to negotiate special deals with the consumer marketplace publishers. Good luck. I have not heard a lot of success stories here, at least so far.

An interesting model there is to look at the way Blockbuster and other video rental stores negotiated deals with the videocassette industry, and where the libraries have ended up in terms of providing access to video content relative to these commercial "libraries." It seems likely that we could see commercial "rental libraries" for ebooks, and it's not clear that real libraries want to go this route. So where does that leave libraries as institutions that manage and provide access to the cultural and intellectual record?

First let me give you the good news. Right now as far as ebooks, it's not that big of a deal. It is not that big of a deal because ebooks mimic printed books in a very literal way. It may be a serious annoyance from a service point of view that you can't deliver ebooks circulated onto patrons' reading devices. But from the point of view of capturing and exercising stewardship over an intellectual record, that record is still there in print. And as long as consumer ebooks are mostly literal translations of things that are dual published in print it is not going to be that critical. Furthermore, I think this is going to be a non-issue for scholarly material by and large.

The primary market for scholarly literature is research libraries. There is a shared interest–indeed a requirement–in developing a mutually advantageous framework for making digital books that are targeted for the scholarly marketplace work, technically and economically. This will happen, just as it has happened with scholarly journals as they have migrated to digital form; it will involve some negotiation, and will take some time to mature. But I am absolutely confident that it will be worked out.

But libraries are not a major market force in the consumer marketplace, and there is precious little motivation for consumer publishing organizations to accommodate libraries. As consumer material begins, when and if it does, to diverge substantially in digital form from its print sources, we are going to start facing some very real issues about our ability to capture, manage, and preserve that part of our intellectual record.

But I also think honestly that the whole business about consumer ebooks is a little bit over hyped. Maybe a lot over hyped. I think there is a fundamental message that we need to be more conscious of as we look at digital books more broadly. What has pushed the move of books to digital form is the ingenuity and curiosity of authors in exploiting the digital medium to communicate and document thinking more effectively. That's what is driving them to do it. That is why these people are experimenting with the intellectual descendants of the monograph in the digital environment. That's why teachers and educators are interested in what we can do to make more effective textbooks by taking them digital.

I think we are most likely to be able to exploit those potentials, at least in today's exploratory era, in a relatively unfettered digital environment; an environment that is not heavily constrained by rights management or by the sort of processor or display that you need to make a cheap consumer electronics box; an environment that lets authors easily, lavishly and even occasionally wastefully exploit the capability of the network information environment. For connectivity, rich linkage, and interaction are the kinds of things that I think may really drive a lot of the most compelling migration of books to digital content. And those are places where I think libraries need to be extremely active in tracking, acquiring, preserving, and furthering the adoption of the book as it moves to its digital form. Because these are the places where the digital book may make a real difference to the quality of human communication.

AUTHOR NOTE

At the time that I gave this presentation, I was working on a lengthy formal article on digital books broadly, which appeared as "The Battle to Define the Future of the Book in the Digital World" in the June, 2001 issue of *First Monday* (www.firstmonday. org). This paper may also be of interest to readers seeking a more extensive exploration of many of the topics discussed here.

Taming Disruptive Technologies, or How to Remain Relevant in the Digital Age

Philip Blackwell

In July 1993, a cartoon appeared in *The New Yorker* depicting a dog seated in front of a computer screen, remarking to another dog, "On the internet, nobody knows you're a dog." This simple cartoon reflected a significant shift in our attitude toward online communication. The Internet had become a part of the popular culture. No longer the province of geeky scientists in cluttered offices and obscure laboratories, the Internet was well known enough to find its way into a popular humor magazine.[1]

Similarly last year, when Stephen King produced the first mass-market novel published exclusively on the Internet, another paradigm shift occurred. King has been followed by scores of other popular authors, each with his own variation on pricing and payment. None has found huge profits waiting at the end of the online rainbow, but none has given it up either.

The world has discovered electronic books, with all their possibilities and shortcomings. E-books have been circling about libraries and academic institutions for several years, but Stephen King focused the lens of popular culture on the e-book, and widened the audience for the debate on the future of print books and bricks and mortar libraries.

Harvard Business School professor Clayton Christensen coined the term disruptive technologies in his influential book, *The Innovator's*

Philip Blackwell is Group Chief Executive, Blackwell Limited.

[Haworth co-indexing entry note]: "Taming Disruptive Technologies, or How to Remain Relevant in the Digital Age." Blackwell, Philip. Co-published simultaneously in *Journal of Library Administration* (The Haworth Information Press, an imprint of The Haworth Press, Inc.) Vol. 35, No. 3, 2001, pp. 33-49; and: *Impact of Digital Technology on Library Collections and Resource Sharing* (ed: Sul H. Lee) The Haworth Information Press, an imprint of The Haworth Press, Inc., 2001, pp. 33-49. Single or multiple copies of this article are available for a fee from The Haworth Document Delivery Service [1-800-HAWORTH, 9:00 a.m. - 5:00 p.m. (EST). E-mail address: getinfo@haworthpressinc.com].

33

Dilemma.[2] E-books are an example of a disruptive technology, that is, a technology that has great appeal to its users but upsets the traditional models. Difficulty coping with disruptive technologies is what explains the problems big companies like IBM and Digital Equipment have had in adapting their values and their processes to the new economies. Because the pace of change is so rapid, even a "new-economy" company like Intel is in danger of becoming the next IBM.

An editorial in the Sunday 8 October 2000, *New York Times* by Paul Krugman talks about the idea of "creative destruction," a phrase first used by Joseph Schumpeter, an Austrian economist.[3] Creative destruction is a result of the continual change caused by technological development. "Destruction," "disruption"–not pleasant words or ones we often think about in connection with our place in the information industry. The other side of disrupting is sustaining, and the other side of destroying is creating. Remaining relevant–for libraries, for vendors, for IBM, or anyone else–means turning disruption and destruction into sustaining creativity. That's our challenge and that's what we mean to do.

E-book technology raises a myriad of questions for traditional publishers, questions that were pretty much sorted out in the print world:

- Who is responsible for content management in the e-book world? E-books require different editorial decisions. In the print world we had "editions" of books. Now they are becoming more like "versions" similar to software. Who is responsible for version control?
- Who hosts the data, catalogs the books, organizes collections and provides a user interface? Who is going to manage the new types of searching tools and indexes that are made possible in an electronic world?
- What about rights management? The electronic book environment makes the copyright issues in journal publishing look almost simple. The intellectual property rights of any given book may be divided between authors, publishers, photographers, artists, agencies, etc.

Closely related to the digital rights management issue is the pricing and ownership debate:

- Are e-books really databases?
- Is a license agreement more appropriate than an outright sale? What happens to the digital files when the license is no longer valid?

- Does an e-book go out of print?
- What happens to the publisher's traditional economic model when print-on-demand technology moves libraries from the "just-in-case" to "just-in-time" model of acquisitions?
- What if the publisher goes out of business?
- What happens if a publisher grants a license to an aggregator and the aggregator sells to someone else? If netLibrary were sold to Amazon, would Amazon own the rights to the books netLibrary licensed from publishers?

Can we take this disruptive technology and tame it? Can we find answers to these questions by finding new ways of doing things, by adapting our processes and our values to accommodate new ways of doing business? This isn't easy. Our established values and familiar processes are exactly what have made us successful in the past. We encourage our colleagues and our employees to behave in ways that are consistent. We want people to use processes that are well designed and proven to work well. Adapting a disruptive technology means that established ways are set aside and new processes are embraced.

BACKGROUND

Let's step back for a moment and examine where the 500 years of a sustaining print technology has brought us. Because I'm a book person, and my company has 120 years of experience supplying books to scholars and libraries, it's important for me to reiterate my belief that in spite of all the excitement, print books are not going away. Some projections for the future of print[4]:

- The Book Industry Study Group, a U.S. trade association specializing in statistics and standards for the book industry, projects a 5% gain in book sales in 2000.
- Total book sales are projected to increase 5.2% in 2000 to an estimated U.S. $24.71 billion, according to forecasts in Book Industry Study Group Trends 2000. If revenue growth hits the forecast target, it will better the 4.3% growth rate posted in 1999.
- While the largest increase is expected to be in the children's book market (thank you, Harry Potter) the second largest sales increase in 2000 is forecast for the college segment with sales projected to increase 8.1% to $3.38 billion. Expanding enrollment combined

with generous public funding are expected to result in a 5.6% increase in sales in this segment this year to $3.61 billion.

- Sales of professional books are projected to increase 5.4% to almost $5 billion and sales in the university press category are estimated to increase 4.8% to $431.5 million. Overall, in the next five years, BISG predicts that book sales will grow at a rate of 5.1% and will reach $30 billion in 2004.

Clearly the book business has considerable life left in it. But new technologies happen, in spite of the fact that we may be perfectly happy with the old. That's the very definition of a disruptive technology. The old ink on paper model has been the technology that has sustained us for the last 500 years. And now the world is going digital. E-books will not supplant print books, at least not for a very long time. But they will find a place on our virtual shelves–along with music, photographs and videos.

THE CHANGING CLIMATE

A poll released in January 2000, commissioned by netLibrary and Yankelovich Partners, reports on the online habits of 2,060 full-time American college and university students. Ninety-three percent of the students surveyed claimed that finding information online makes more sense than going to the library or bookstore, and yet an even higher percentage (98 percent) indicated that they buy textbooks at the campus bookstore and use the library to do research.[5]

Research conducted by the University of Texas in Austin revealed that books in the library's electronic collection circulate on average 5 times per book per month. Comparable titles in the undergraduate library's print collection circulate on average 1.1 times per year. Even the most popular of the print collection books circulate only 12-15 times per year.[6]

If there is anything holding students back from adopting e-books, it's likely to be price. Students tend to show a preference for free e-books, or if not free, those that are subsidized by the library. The University of Virginia made 1,200 of its 50,000 online texts available at no charge in August 2000 to enthusiastic response. The program attracts a broad range of users: leisure readers, high schoolers and university students from more than 100 countries have downloaded books. The e-books can be downloaded to PCs and handheld devices, and use Microsoft's Clear Type technology. The digital library is accessed 90,000 times a day, by approximately 25,000 users–making it the busiest public e-book library in the world.[7]

No question that among young readers, the climate is right for an e-book solution. Yet like any emerging industry, the field is confused and confusing.

E-books fall into one of four distinct types:

1. *Downloadable to the user's PC.* The advantage to this type is that no special hardware is required. The disadvantages are the time it takes to download, and the fact that most readers do not enjoy reading a book from a computer screen. Studies have shown that if electronic documents exceed two pages, most people will download it. The distribution of these books is difficult to control, so most are books already in the public domain.

2. *Accessible on the Web, but not downloadable.* These books can be purchased or "borrowed" (the netLibrary model) but they do not remain on the reader's PC. These books are more likely to be copyrighted works, with royalties flowing back to the owners.

3. *Downloadable to a reader device.* The devices are usually hand-held with high quality screen resolution. They have features designed to make reading them appear similar to a print book (bookmarking and margin notes) as well as sophisticated features not available in a print book (keyword searching, sizable fonts, back lighting, linked dictionaries and thesauri). The major disadvantage is the expense of these devices. Also, the readers are still not as portable or as pleasurable to read as print books. They are bulky. Battery life is too short. And perhaps the most annoying, various readers on the market are not compatible with one another and have different downloadable title lists–making the purchase of multiple readers a must for libraries that wish to offer a wide selection.

4. *Print-on-Demand* is a final category of e-books, meant to be read on paper rather than electronically. Print on demand books are stored digitally and printed on a high-speed and high-quality printer as the need arises.

E-book reader devices abound–any list of them is outdated the moment it's completed:

- Adobe Glassbook
- Gemstar REB

- Everybook
- E-bookMan
- Microsoft Reader

Early electronic books were simply scanned and digitized using optical character recognition. In recent years propriety software has been developed to handle graphics and preserve formatting–Adobe's Portable Document Format (PDF) and Microsoft's ClearType™ being the two most prominent competing formats. And as usual with a new technology, there are competing standards, i.e., Open e-Book and EBX™ Electronic Book Exchange.

New business models are emerging to offer publishers of electronic books services tailored to the digital environment. Data warehousing, digitizing and digital rights management are offered by businesses such as Versaware, netLibrary, Lightning Source, iUniverse and other new players in this field. Companies such as Reciprocal, SofLock, and Content Guard have developed new businesses around digital rights management, changing the concept of intellectual property protection from a legal service to a technology product.

The value chain for e-books and print-on-demand is dynamic and volatile. Watching it sort itself out is exciting and dizzying. New printing technology has made it financially viable for publishers to print out a single book, rather than risk the inefficiencies and costs associated with large print runs and unsold books. Companies such as Lightning Source provide end-to-end digital fulfillment services, ranging from content conversion, management and storage to the distribution of printed "on demand" books. A title can be delivered any time, anywhere in any available format the end user wants.

Print-on-demand allows the library to adopt the same "just in time" versus "just in case" philosophy for book acquisition that the rapid growth of document delivery services in the nineties made possible for journal publishing. Indeed there are economic advantages for publishers in the just-in-time model, but there are enormous risks. What happens to first-copy costs when the first copy is followed by a one-at-a-time print run of uncertain size? What happens to the price of the book when print runs shrink to tens rather than tens-of-thousands?

So what does this mean for traditional book distributors? How do traditional vendors continue to add value to a world rushing to digital. The answer is to continue to do what we do best: provide distribution services for publishers, acquisition solutions for libraries, and ease of access for readers. We are in the service business. Content is the tangible deliverable, and it's available from a variety of sources. As alternatives to the traditional print book begin to appear, variety in format naturally becomes part of the service.

Tim O'Reilly of O'Reilly Publishing talks about the "ecology of digital publishing." O'Reilly suggests that in the e-book world distributors are more important than ever. The numbers of books published multiplied by the number of users will make direct sales impossible. In the early days of the Web, everyone figured it would "disintermediate" everything. But this has proven to be untrue. E-business remains business, and the same models hold true. Businesses that deal directly with customers will continue to do so. Those that require distributors to reach the broad range of customers will continue to do so. The same models that hold true in the physical world will work in the e-world. Large aggregators will have the biggest chunks of the business.[8]

HOW WE SERVE OUR MARKETS

The First Stakeholder: The User

Most of what is written and said about e-books today addresses publisher concerns–how to protect intellectual property, how to manage the rights issues, and most important of all, how to protect the prevalent economic model or replace it with a model that is equally viable.

What is missing in these conversations often seems to be this: what does the user want? The reader is the ultimate consumer. What format, what device, what distribution model, licensing agreement, what pricing model addresses the needs of the user? Until we start answering those questions, nothing else really counts.

We should know by now that designing products and services that meet only the needs of the shareholders is never successful. E-books are enjoying a popularity bred of novelty, curiosity, and perhaps wishful thinking. Librarians really want an e-book solution. The "if-it-doesn't-exist-on-the-Web-it-doesn't-exist" student demands it. Yet very little of the rhetoric about e-books really addresses the customer requirements.

Napster got it partly right. It's democratic, easy to use, and suggests that the prevailing music publishing distribution and pricing models are outdated and over-priced. The 20 million or so Napster users could generate over $2.4 billion dollars a year (at $10/month) and most have indicated a willingness to pay. The problem is the owners, clinging to old ways of doing business, refuse to sell. Software companies such as Reciprocal, ContentGuard and Soflock are coming up with digital rights management technology that allows a "Napster-like" distribution model which feeds revenues back to the publisher.

What else does the user want? This is an area that needs more research because mostly what we know so far is that the user wants e-books. What else?

Aggregation

High on everyone's list is the ability to reach multiple publisher servers through a single, common interface, organized by all the standard search keys, i.e., author, title, subject, publisher, format, isbn, etc. The netLibrary research found that 90% of e-book users want the ability to search across the contents of a single book, and 80% want searching across the content of collections of e-books.

Powerful Searching with Subject Access

Publisher collections are really not of much interest. As Cliff Lynch has pointed out, nobody ever goes to the library to visit the Elsevier room or the Taylor & Francis collection. Right now most of the aggregating of e-books is technologically based, organized by the digitizer, rather than editorially by subject. There is no single source for metadata on e-books, and no way to search across the entire e-book universe by topic.

Disaggregation and Pay-Per-View

In time, powerful search engines will make it possible to search across a variety of databases and servers. Users want the ability to piece together their own "books" comprised of chapters, sections, paragraphs or even sentences from a variety of sources. And they don't want to buy the entire book to get to the part they will use.

Portability

Users want e-book models that exploit the value of the Web, but are not tied to the desktop. Creating an online reader with the portability and elegance of the print book is a technological challenge, but it will happen. The same netLibrary research mentioned above among current e-book users suggests that 60% prefer to print and read e-books offline. This will change as the technology improves.

The Second Stakeholder: The Librarian

We also know some things that libraries want. Libraries have embraced the netLibrary model because it was, and still is, the first and most widely available e-book service. netLibrary has done a remarkable job of creating a brand for itself and building an impressive collection of electronic books in a very short time. They've done this by spending money on the finest technology, talented people and very savvy marketing. The netLibrary model isn't perfect, and much of what they have done to make publishers comfortable with their products are the very things that make libraries unhappy, e.g., the one-book/one-user model. netLibrary took the brave step of being the first in the marketplace, and through their experience, we've all learned a lot. Blackwell's has partnered with netLibrary and represents them in the academic market. Through this channel, we've had the chance on a daily basis to talk with librarians about what they want from e-books.

What we've learned:

Collection Development

The purchase of e-books should proceed along the same collection development avenues that librarians use to select print books. Most libraries are purchasing e-books to supplement their print collections. E-books provide a way for library users to have access to materials in a different format, but those materials still must support the basic research and curriculum needs of the parent institution.

Multiple Users

While the one-book/one-user model is easy to understand and mimics the print book model, it does not exploit the inherent value of online access. The power of the Web is that it allows one-to-many viewing of electronic texts. The restriction of one-to-one seems artificial and unreasonable to librarians and users. Ideally librarians would like 24-hour/7-day per week unlimited simultaneous access, but they know that's unlikely to happen.

Flexible Validation and Authentication

Librarians don't want to be in the password administration business. Internet technology gives us the ability to validate users in ways that are effective and unobtrusive. It also allows for access to be given to users wherever they may be located. Librarians are struggling with providing services to remote users and distance learners. E-books are perfectly suited to this purpose, as long as there are no barriers to the authentication of remote users.

Integration into the Library Catalog

Bibliographic records for e-books must be integrated into the library's online public access catalogs. Nothing promotes use of electronic materials more effectively than this linked access. For this reason, libraries want their e-books delivered with MARC records and tables of contents.

Workflow Integration

Librarians want to order e-books using the same workflows they use for print books. This means both inclusion in approval plans and book-by-book purchases through EDI, Collection Manager, or any other avenue in current use. Librarians like the ability to purchase ready-made collections, but the collections cannot be limited to any one provider–e.g., netLibrary–or to one publisher either.

Copyright Clearance

Librarians are among the most law-abiding people on the planet. Librarians fight for the interests of their users through unwavering support for fair-use policies. But at the end of the day, librarians want to respect the rights of the owners of intellectual property, because they understand that those protections are what stimulates the sharing of insight and discovery. They are asking for rights management systems that are fair, comprehensible and allow for easy compliance.

Understandable Pricing Models

Different materials are used in different ways. Among the pricing models librarians would like to see are:

- Pay-per-view
- Per book with perpetual access (similar to print books)
- Subscription/license with or without perpetual access
- Rental (for titles of short term interest, e.g., computer books)
- Mix-and-match pricing

Standardized Technology. Librarians are concerned with the costs of maintaining the infrastructures needed for digital libraries. Libraries cannot afford to support multiple, non-compatible formats, to buy a variety of non-compatible reading devices, and teach users how to navigate proliferating search engines and user interfaces. The world is a messy place, and it will never be possible to have one-true-perfect solution. That would mean the end of progress. However, we are all well-served when the technologies are compatible, the systems inter-operable, and the products integrated.

The Third Stakeholder: The Publisher

Blackwell's has an active publisher relations program for all three parts of the business–library services, retail, and online. And of course, within the family are two well known publishing houses, Blackwell Science and Blackwell Publishers. It's not surprising then, that we spend considerable time talking to publishers. We know that in the area of electronic books, publishers have more questions than answers. The disruptive technology, that I mentioned earlier, is very real to them. Publishers have sustaining technologies that have served them well for many years. E-books represent enormous disruption to the established models.

Our publishing colleagues look to us for help in finding solutions. Many of the services we provide publishers in the print world will transfer relatively easily to the digital one. Some will not, and some new services will be required.

What we know so far is that publishers want some of what we already do for print:

Aggregation of Orders

Library supply vendors exist to aggregate orders to publishers from a great number of single libraries into larger and more efficient batches. Micro-transactions derived from individual library sales are an expensive problem for publishers. The shipping of physical objects goes away in the e-book environment, but the micro-transactions remain. The other value added services provided by the library supply vendor–alerting, invoicing, claiming and payment, customer service–are unchanged in the digital environment.

Integration into Approval Plans

Most approval plans today combine multiple formats of titles–hardcover; paperback or CD ROMs. Having e-books included in those plans is a natural evolutionary step and creates a guaranteed market for publishers.

Advance Alerting Services

Blackwell's sends out hundreds of thousands of new title announcements to customers throughout the world. E-notes is a new service that provides electronic notification in place of paper forms. It is in fact a very sophisticated email alerting service. Including e-books in these announcements is a planned enhancement for the service.

Inclusion in Web-Based Customer Facing Products

Collection Manager and Blackwell's Online Bookshop (BOB) are products that disintermediate the order process and allow librarians, students and scholars to locate and order books. Blackwell's Online Bookshop leverages the brand recognition of Blackwell's into a market wider than the traditional Blackwell's Book Services market, and provides the academic user with an attractive alternative to Amazon. Including e-books in these products is a natural. In the spring of 2001, Blackwell's customers will be able to find and order netLibrary titles through Collection Manager.

Sales and Marketing

In addition to our New Title Announcement Service, Blackwell's has a world-wide sales force out selling books to libraries. Because of our partnership with netLibrary, they sell both print books and e-books. As other partnerships are forged, other e-book publishers and distributors will also benefit from this sales network.

Blackwell's is known in the industry for its special offers and cooperative publisher promotions. In the past 4 years our sales in this area have increased by 300%. And these sales extend to e-books as well as print books. Earlier this year, we did a joint promotion with netLibrary of the Choice Magazine Outstanding Academic Titles available as e-books.

Cataloging Records and TOCs

We've noted above the importance of including bibliographic records in the library's online public access catalog. Librarians will buy more e-books only if the ones they have are actually used. Blackwell's MaRC with Books service provides bibliographic records to hundreds of libraries. When library records are enhanced with Blackwell's Table of Contents data, studies have shown that circulation increases by as much as 50%. Early e-book adopters have noted that including bibliographic records for e-books similarly causes usage of the materials to spike dramatically.

Profitability

In this area, publishers want what they've always wanted. Increased revenue streams and lower costs. Publishers are attracted to potential savings through lower physical production costs, cheaper distribution and fewer returns.

Publishers also need some services we do not provide:

Content Management

Publishers would like to exploit the power of the Web to provide access to materials at the chapter, section, page and even word level. They recognize that the more accessible, i.e., the more sophisticated the search retrieval, the more their books will be used. Nevertheless publishers want to retain their own branding and don't want their rich valuable content to be used as "bait"–a loss leader for other content of lower quality. They stress the need to brand the content, not the site–for example, the way the "Dummies books" are branded wherever they appear. Some suggest that their logo must appear on every page.

Most publishers are evaluating the options for creating their own websites, but the experience of electronic journals has taught us all that aggregation is what works for the user.

Security and Digital Rights Management

Publishers would like to insure that text delivered on-screen would be protected from copying and pasting. Also, they would like to be confident that when a complete e-book is sold to a library or individual, it would be impossible for the purchaser to make multiple copies–at least without additional permission and/or payment. There are many models for doing both, but it is in everyone's interest to maintain a balance between protecting content and making sure the reader is able to use the material effectively and with at least as much ease as he has with the printed book. Controlling the use of content too vigorously may discourage the development of the market, or even worse, promote the growth of the electronic "black market."

As noted above, most library customers are not out to break the rules. Most would readily pay and follow the rules if they are allowed to do so via clear presentation of the rules and easy-to-use methods for clearance and payment. Effective digital rights management actually encourages compliance. Digital rights management could be looked at as a way to sell content in a way never possible before, and after all, publishing is all about getting content used and getting paid for it. Only unauthorized copying is the problem.

Digital File Hosting

Most publishers do not have the infrastructure, capability, or knowledge to digitize, tag, store, and deliver their own electronic content. And most are unsure whether to develop this capability internally, do it in partnership with someone else, or outsource it entirely.

Have We Learned Anything from E-Journals?

In a hundred years when we look back at the development of electronic books and journals there will be no perceivable time difference between the arrival of the e-journal and the arrival of the e-book. But as we look at developments today, it appears to us that the e-journal's been around for quite some time, and therefore we may be able to learn some lessons there. Yet most of what we know simply confirms what we've already guessed. There is no one clear model.

Hosting. No standard has emerged for the hosting of electronic journals. The library community appears to have settled into some combination of publisher hosting (Elsevier), subscription vendor hosting (Swetsnet navigator), third-party hosting (ingenta, CatchWord) and/or hosting by the library itself (OhioLink).

Pricing. Likewise, no single payment model has emerged. The two prevailing options are subscription licensing and pay-per-view. The subscription model might be:

- the cost of the paper plus a percentage for the electronic version
- the electronic version free with the purchase of a paper subscription
- a subscription for the online only–either discounted or not from the price of the paper subscription.

Pay-per-view options still are predominantly the domain of document delivery services or re-packaging services such as Northern Light.

Aggregation. Like the e-book reader, the goal of the e-journal user searching online is to find full text, not just a pointer to it. Services that aggregate titles must lead eventually to the text itself. With journals, the citation may be discovered a variety of ways–through a traditional periodical index, an online subject index, a table of contents service, or an electronic journal collection. Depending on the hosting model, the text can be delivered a variety of ways too–from the publisher server, from the subscription agent or third party host, or sometimes even from another library.

CAN VENDORS TAME THE DISRUPTIVE TECHNOLOGY AND REMAIN RELEVANT?

The answer is yes. Many vendors have a big history of working with scholars, librarians and publishers. We hear from you often, and we listen well. Right now, we see ourselves as navigators. We understand the needs of libraries and the commercial imperatives of publishers. We are positioned at the nexus of libraries and publishers and we offer our interpretive services to both sides.

There are core competencies that we offer, and as noted above, these will not change in the digital environment:

- Aggregation of orders
- Creation of bibliographic databases
- Provision of cataloging records
- Table of contents delivery
- Approval plans and alerting services
- Invoicing
- Customer service
- Standing order management

There are new services that we must learn how to provide–solutions to content management, licensing and access management, hosting and digital rights. Some of these we may do on our own, and others in partnerships with companies that have competencies we do not.

Blackwell's is not primarily a technology company. We do not see ourselves developing software for digital rights management, maintaining servers for the hosting of large data files, or developing complex Web search engines. But we know how to forge alliances with people who do those things well. We know the middle man position well and can add value to both sides by positioning ourselves in the middle.

In the future an e-book transaction for the library might look like this:

The librarian locates a title through the vendor website. He sends the order to the vendor, either alone or in a batch of orders for other titles, both print and electronic. The vendor's sourcing system locates the title on a Versaware, netLibrary or publisher server. The vendor places the order on behalf of the library, indicating the format in which the file should be supplied. A third party digital rights management system authenticates the user, assesses whatever payment is necessary to clear the rights, and provides the digital unlocking device. If the library maintains its own digital library server, the host then "ships" the e-book file to the library address. If not, access is validated for the library on the host server of the publisher or data warehouser. These instructions are sent with the order based on rules already established in the library's customer profile.

Once the transaction is complete, the vendor sends the library a TOC enhanced MARC record for the title and an invoice, which includes the price of the book, a royalty fee if appropriate, and a fee for other services supplied (e.g., the enhanced MARC record). The vendor is invoiced by the publisher.

Approval plans and alerting services would operate in much the same way, using advance information supplied by the e-book publisher.

Over time, as the technology changes, as libraries change, as publishing changes, these processes will change. The market will determine which of the many pricing models will survive. Our goal is to stay very close to our two primary constituents–libraries and publishers–and listen well to what you tell us. Transforming disruptive technologies into sustaining technologies requires understanding where the new technology improves the old and what pieces of the old technology must be maintained.

Remaining relevant means taming the disruptive technology beast. It means finding and nurturing that sustaining creativity. Blackwell's has no intention of becoming the Digital Equipment Corporation of the book industry. We have many questions. We know some of the answers, and we are actively examining those things we've yet to sort out.

Few are suggesting that e-books will replace print. The two media will co-exist for a long time. And the possibilities for using the two technologies in a complementary fashion are exciting and motivating. That's what keeps us relevant and that's what we intend to do for a very long time.

NOTES

1. *The New Yorker*, July 1993.
2. Christensen, Clayton C., *The Innovator's Dilemma*, Harvard Business School Press, 1997.
3. Krugman, Paul, "Reckonings; Create and Destroy," *The New York Times*, editorial, Sunday, October 8, 2000.
4. Book Industry Study Group, *Book Industry Trends 2000: Covering the Years 1994-2004*, prepared for the Book Industry Study Group by Fordham University Graduate School of Business Administration, 2000.
5. Yankelovich Partners Study of Online Habits of American College Students. Commissioned by netLibrary. <http://www.netlibrary.com/press_releases/january132000-1.asp>.
6. Unpublished research. Private email communication to the author.
7. University of Virginia Digital Library website <http://www.lva.lib.va.us/dlp/index.htm>.
8. Remarks at "Digital Rights Management and Digital Distribution for Publishing," held August 14-17, 2000, Oxford, United Kingdom.

APPENDIX

Other Useful Websites:

All About e-Books
http://aalbc.com/e-books/Allaboute-books.htm

e-Booknet.com
http://www.e-booknet.com/

e-Books.org
http://e-books.org/

Know Better.com
http://knowbetter.com/

Bibliofuture: electronic book readers and libraries
http://www.bibliofuture.homepage.com/

Going "Electronic-Only":
Early Experiences and Issues

Karen Hunter

INTRODUCTION

Libraries, journal publishers and authors now have more than a decade of experience with electronic versions of traditional paper journals. What began as experiments in the late 1980s and first half of the 1990s evolved into commercial offerings of digital journals. While there are some journals that were "born digital" and have never had a paper version and many paper journals that have yet to go digital, the majority of major research journals now have both paper and electronic editions.

When electronic editions began to parallel paper, it added a burden to both librarians and publishers, as both had to maintain two systems, with their associated costs. The burden was borne because of the hoped-for benefits associated with electronic delivery, including increased functionality, desktop delivery, faster access. A frequent underlying question became: when will the community shift to "electronic only"? While I am not aware of any paper-plus-electronic journal that has yet stopped its paper edition, an increasing number of publishers do offer an "electronic-only" option and the number of libraries (and individuals) choosing this option is growing.

Karen Hunter is Senior Vice President, Elsevier Science, 655 Sixth Avenue, New York, NY 10010 (E-mail: k.hunter@elsevier.com).

[Haworth co-indexing entry note]: "Going "Electronic-Only": Early Experiences and Issues." Hunter, Karen. Co-published simultaneously in *Journal of Library Administration* (The Haworth Information Press, an imprint of The Haworth Press, Inc.) Vol. 35, No. 3, 2001, pp. 51-65; and: *Impact of Digital Technology on Library Collections and Resource Sharing* (ed: Sul H. Lee) The Haworth Information Press, an imprint of The Haworth Press, Inc., 2001, pp. 51-65. Single or multiple copies of this article are available for a fee from The Haworth Document Delivery Service [1-800-HAWORTH, 9:00 a.m. - 5:00 p.m. (EST). E-mail address: getinfo@haworthpressinc.com].

This paper addresses publishers' decisions to create an electronic-only option, librarians' decisions to subscribe to electronic-only versions, the issues and concerns of both and the outlook for the future.

PUBLISHERS' PERSPECTIVES

In deciding to offer an electronic version of their journals, most publishers–perhaps all publishers–are motivated by the increased functionality of the electronic version and, therefore, the competitive need to produce this product. The competition is, in the first instance, for the attention of readers. By extension, it is for authors. The argument goes that if the journal is not available internationally on the desktop, it will have fewer readers, and fewer readers ultimately means you lose key authors and editors.

A decision is therefore made to invest in the editorial, production, marketing and administrative infrastructure to support an electronic version in parallel with the paper. There is initially little thought of cost-savings that might eventually flow from electronic journals, as that "eventually" seems too far away to contemplate. As is now well-understood, in order for publishers to harvest significant cost-savings, they have to stop printing entirely. The "first copy" costs associated with going on press are fixed and for many scholarly publishers there are few savings if the print run is cut by a few or even a few hundred copies.

Individual Subscribers

There are exceptions, however, and one of those exceptions provided one of the first incentives for a publisher to offer "electronic only" access. That exception was the savings to be gained if a significant number of individual society members chose to receive their member journal(s) electronically rather than in paper. The first experiments with offering electronic versions were made when CD-ROM drives first became common on PCs. Delivery was not necessarily as rapid as in paper–perhaps a quarterly CD–but the thought of not getting all that paper and having something searchable was appealing to many scientists. The conversion had begun.

When the Web became the delivery method of choice, more societies offered members the choice of paper or electronic and an increasing number of individuals chose electronic. For example, ASIS & T (The American Society for Information Science & Technology) follows the pattern of many societies in giving members the paper vs. electronic option with no difference in member rates. The American Physical Society offers individuals $25 online-only subscriptions for its titles and has thousands of individuals subscibing.[1] Acceptance of this option has not been as rapid in fields highly dependent on the quality of the graphics reproduction (e.g., some areas of medicine).

While the option to take electronic over paper will appeal to many individuals, it is not clear how societies will handle long-term access by these individuals. Do you have access to all available years so long as you are a member? Do you have access only to the current year? The individual may have to make an archiving trade-off: do I give up the nuisance of maintaining my paper copies and go e-only, knowing that there may come a time when I no longer have access to those electronic files?

Institutional Subscribers

Offering electronic-only access to institutional subscribers has been a more gradual process, but now many publishers provide this option. In general, this offering has been in response to libraries' expressed interest in being able to get electronic-only. That is, it is in response to market demand, not a push on the publisher's part.

At Elsevier, electronic-only has been available for several years, with a modest discount from the standard print + electronic price. Initially, there was no one taking this option. But by 2000, regional patterns began to occur. Fully 50% of the revenues from Australia are now from electronic-only subscribers, a large number of Swedish university libraries have chosen e-only (within a consortium environment), and there are e-only subscribers appearing elsewhere in the world, including the U.S. and the UK.

The American Institute of Physics has also offered this option for three years. In 1999, 0.1% of the institutional subscribers took the option. In 2000, it grew to 1%. Early returns for 2001 suggested there could be as many as 10% of the institutions opting for electronic-only, but it tapered off and a final number of between 3% and 5% is expected.[2] An e-only subscription is 30% less expensive than the AIP paper price.

The American Physical Society began offering electronic-only subscriptions in 2001, at a 15% discount from the print plus electronic price. As of February, 2001, 55 institutions had selected this option.[3] APS noted that industrial laboratories have been early adopters, as they do not consider themselves to be archival repositories. Elsevier had expected the same pattern among its corporate libraries for the same reason, but its largest corporate customers (pharmaceutical companies) have so far retained paper, as they say their researchers still want to have the paper available.

Academic Press made a more fundamental conversion for its electronic customers. It said that the principal payment was for the electronic version and that paper copies would then be available at a modest additional charge. This is the model that some libraries advocate, as evidenced from advice Elsevier has received from its library advisory boards. It is, perhaps, the inevitable model for the future. There are problems to be worked out, however, including (1) tax issues (some states have sales taxes on electronic products and there are punitive VAT charges in Europe, where electronic subscriptions are subject to a very high tax and paper subscriptions are not), (2) the unwillingness of some governments (notably Japan) to fund the purchase of anything that is not tangible, and (3) the relationship with subscription agents.

Agent Relationships

The agent issue is a non-trivial one for all participants in the journals acquisition process. Agents have traditionally played an important role in journal purchasing. They offered a definitive source of information about journals, provided consolidated ordering and billing and handled the currency transactions for libraries purchasing internationally. This has been an increasingly complicated and technology-intensive business, leading (as with publishing) to consolidation. For their services, they had two main sources of income: (1) a discount from many publishers (however, some publishers–notably some societies–refused to discount) and (2) a service charge to the library (who is their customer). With paper journals, as many as 90% of a commercial publisher's orders could come through subscription agents, with the larger agents providing the renewal information in machine-readable form, improving efficiency and accuracy.

With the introduction of electronic subscriptions, the picture became more complicated. For a publisher who offers its electronic editions as an automatic feature for paper subscribers, there may be little interruption of agent relationships. Elsevier Science, for example, offers its Web editions program to institutional paper subscribers. This is a free current awareness service giving access to the most recent twelve months of a subscribed-to title. The paper order continues with the agent and the library can sign an online, click-through license to turn on the Web editions.

For access to Elsevier Science's more comprehensive (archival) ScienceDirect, however, the library enters into license negotiations directly with our account managers. Many factors enter into that negotiation, including favorable terms associated with long term commitments. It is important that we, as the publisher, are talking directly with our customers, as we need to understand their situation and priorities. These are complex negotiations that cannot be delegated to a subscription agent. So long as the paper subscriptions continue, the agent is involved. But what if the decision is made to go e-only? In theory, the agent no longer has a role. In practice, that means that much of the day-to-day, title-by-title renewal process will move from the agent to the publisher. The publisher's back office must be prepared to handle this.

Early experiences at Elsevier remind us that this is not as easy as one might think. Some of the very basic steps we needed to take (such as organizing refunds for paper copies already renewed by new e-only subscribers) were not smoothly handled at the start. Elsevier is certainly not unique in having had such problems. Nor are we unique in seeking to improve back office systems for the future, for example, adding customer-specific URLs with online holdings information and Internal renewals. What is clear is that significant resources have to be committed to the back office processes and the benefits that could be offered by the agent in such electronic-only transactions must be carefully examined.

LIBRARIANS' PERSPECTIVES

In preparing this paper, I invited some of the Elsevier electronic-only library customers to comment on their reasons for choosing that option. I also asked other publishers for their experiences. The pattern of responses is perhaps predictably consistent. Libraries have decided to go e-only for the following reasons:

- Some libraries saw the value in electronic journals–desktop availability, searchability, hopefully earlier access–but could not afford to support both paper and electronic. Therefore, they made the choice for electronic.
- For others, while it may have been possible to support both systems, the ability to save on the subscription cost was sufficient to go e-only.

- There was a desire to save on shelf space and on the costs (direct and indirect) associated with printing and binding. (These are the customers who will be particularly pleased as publishers digitize the backfiles of their journals.)
- For younger institutions, there was less of a paper tradition and the opportunity to "go electronic only" had less resistance.
- Finally, there was a sense that there was "better value for money" with the electronic, particularly in situations where consortial purchasing offered wider access to titles not otherwise available.

I also asked how important it was that other libraries in the region or country still held paper. This touches, of course, on electronic archiving, which is discussed in more detail below, and most responses said that archiving was an important issue in license negotiations. Some libraries indicated that either there was some national resource upon whom they could rely, such as the British Library; however, even in that case there was a concern about electronic archiving at the national level. And it is interesting to note that the first university to sign an electronic-only agreement with Elsevier Science, Macquarie University in Australia, had a provision in its license that the library would receive all 1999 and 2000 back issues in print should the agreement between the two parties be terminated for any reason.[4]

I think the issue of regional paper back-up is more important than might be consciously acknowledged. While making the decision to go electronic-only is not an easy one for any institution, it is made more comfortable by the knowledge that, in case of need, there was a source to whom one could turn to fill a request. It will become more interesting when a national or regional library of last resort decides to be the last one to "turn off the [paper] light" and go electronic-only as well.

Our electronic-only customers were asked if others outside of the library were involved in the decision, specifically users, faculty or university administrators. At the University of Bristol, all three were consulted: "We sought agreement from heads of academic departments and from the University's central administration before going ahead, placed announcements in the University internal newsletter, and raised the issue at meetings of the library user group."[5] Others consulted a steering group and at least one library made the decision solely on the basis of library staff evaluation.

The concerns that libraries had in making the decision to stop receiving paper included the following:

- Researchers might be critical about the loss of paper journals.
- The quality of the electronic product (in this case, Elsevier's on-site service, where the library receives its own copies of the electronic files) and of the server (not from Elsevier) chosen.
- A risk with large consortium agreements that take large parts of library budgets that there will be fewer resources available to build local collections. Non-core material disappears and the collections become more and more similar.
- A concern about what would happen if either the university is unable to afford continued access to ScienceDirect at some time in the future or the company itself ceases to provide the service.
- Concern when an issue on the electronic service is delayed relative to the paper delivery, undermining arguments in favor of online journals.
- Increased pressure on the campus network and on printer provision.
- Need for electronic archival assurances, both as to Elsevier itself and more broadly for an archive held in independent hands.

When the same question was posed to other publishers, the responses were consistent as to archival concerns. However, publishers were of the view that librarians were held back by user resistance. "Librarians state that their older patrons insist on having print available." In the case of physics, there was also some sense of academic conservatism and "a decoupling of the beneficiaries of the price incentive (central libraries) from the decision makers (departmental faculty)."

While it is clearly early to evaluate the decision to go electronic-only, libraries and publishers were asked for their experiences and satisfaction level to date. From the other publishers' perspective, it may be a case of "no news is good news." They have received no complaints thus far. For the Elsevier Science libraries that responded, comments included:

- "All in all, relatively satisfied." Concerns about issues missing or delayed.
- "The experience has been mainly positive. There were critical voices raised as the e-only policy was put into effect. However, due to the fact that the existing collection of print journals was relatively small, the migration to e-only was not so dramatic as it might be for a larger institution."

- "Electronic substitution of print journals can offer a reliable service which is acceptable to the academic community. Print based subscriptions bear little correlation to actual use in a networked environment. Access to the total database, without conditions on use, generates greatly increased usage. Pricing models need to be reappraised to take account of usage patterns. Volume related access to the total database is likely to be a key determinant in any new pricing model. The cost savings to the library in not having to receive and store print based journals is likely to be considerable, although no analysis has yet been made of these potential savings."[6]

Finally, librarians were asked what advice they would give other librarians considering such a move. While Peter King of Bristol said "think twice," others were more positive. Those within the BIBSAM consortium in Sweden offered the following remarks:[7]

- "E-only is sufficient, given the high quality of the product from the vendor."
- "The great advantage with these agreements on a national level is that we, as an individual library, do not have to handle unique titles. We also feel very confident to be able to lean on the legal expertise of BIBSAM."
- "[We] can recommend the e-only way of working with journals. [We] recognize that migration to e-only is probably a lot less problematic for a small, young university than for a large institution with a long history of collection building."
- "The timing of the transition to e-only, in terms of calendar year and renewals of print, is extremely important. In our case, all the libraries that should be e-only from the start of the agreement in January 1999 had already ordered and paid for their print at the time when the agreement was signed. In spite of cancellations during January-March 1999, the printed journals kept coming. The subscription agents were sometimes cooperative in the effort of canceling printed journals, sometimes not."
- "Among the lessons learned: spell out who is responsible for any refund and how it will be administered; make sure both parties understand and agree on the essence of each term."

Neil McLean offered the following conclusion to his paper: "The McQuarie/Elsevier ScienceDirect partnership has challenged traditional library views on collection development, provided momentum for the transition to a networked information service environment and provided 'proof-of-concept' to other university libraries who are now embarking on a similar path."

ELECTRONIC ARCHIVING

As indicated above, one of the critical issues surrounding a decision to go "electronic-only" is whether there will be a trustworthy electronic archive. In what is now several years of talking with library directors and others critical to the future of electronic collections, I have repeatedly heard the statement that it is the archiving issue that most holds back the decision to cancel paper subscriptions. This far outweighs any concerns about user acceptance of electronic. Indeed, one Ivy League university librarian told me that in talking with faculty, approximately 75% were ready to let paper go. But for the librarians, the archiving question has to be solved first.

Because of these concerns of customers, Elsevier Science was among the very first to make a formal archiving commitment. In 1999 our license for ScienceDirect started to carry the following wording:

Basic Policy

1. Elsevier Science (ES) will maintain the digital archive of the journals it owns and makes available through the Service ("ES Journals").
2. It is ES's intention to maintain the digital files of ES Journals in perpetuity, converting them as appropriate if the technology used for storage or access changes. The current format standards are SGML and PDF and most files are being retained in both formats.
3. ES understands that the permanent availability of these archival files is of critical concern to its customers. Therefore, it makes the commitment that, in the unlikely event that neither it nor SD can assume the responsibility for maintaining the archive, it will transfer the archive to one or more depositories mutually acceptable to ES and an independent board of library advisors.
4. ES publishes many journals owned by others (such as scientific societies). To the extent it has the right to do so, ES will include these journals in the Service and will maintain them in its digital archives in the same manner in which it maintains the ES Jour-

nals. Should ES cease to be the publisher for such a journal or cease to have electronic rights, it will use reasonable efforts to ensure that either the archives remain available through the Service or that the owner makes them available on the same access terms via a new host. ES cannot guarantee the permanent availability of journals owned by others.

5. If ES sells or otherwise transfers ownership of an ES Journal to another publisher, it will use reasonable efforts to retain a non-exclusive copy of the digital archive for that title and make it available through the Service to existing Subscribers.

6. If ES ceases publication of an ES Journal, the digital archive will be maintained at ES and be made available through the Service.

The library community reaction was initially very positive about this announcement, but rather soon the concerns about the transfer of the archive to a neutral (i.e., library-controlled) location began to emerge. The promises in 3 above were a start, but there was a feeling that it would be better to have some copies of the archive in library hands now, not simply in the event that we exit the business. At the same time, Elsevier Science was also examining its own internal procedures for maintaining the archive. These were good, but certainly could also be improved and we decided that we, too, would perhaps feel more comfortable with archival copies also in library hands.

The approach that Elsevier has taken has three components:

1. There are perhaps a dozen libraries around the world who presently receive a full set of all of our electronic journals for local installation. While there are not formal archiving agreements with these customers (and one library has said it has no interest in an archiving responsibility), these are de facto archives in the event of a catastrophe. Two of these systems (OhioLINK and the University of Toronto) have indicated a willingness to at least discuss this more formally.

2. Discussions have started with certain national libraries or bodies (such as the Library of Congress and the Royal Library in The Netherlands) about electronic archiving arrangements. Ultimately, a network of such arrangements is anticipated around the world.

3. Elsevier Science is working with Yale University Library on an archival project now in the planning stages under funding from the Mellon Foundation.

It is expected that through these efforts, as well as vigilance internally by Elsevier in maintaining the archive, libraries will soon have the basic reassurance they need to make the decision to go electronic only.

ISSUES AND THE FUTURE

Discontinued Titles

The basic provision for electronic archiving does not, however, remove all of the access concerns. What about when journals change ownership or a publisher loses the contract to publish a society journal? Publishers are just now starting to face those questions and libraries have been confronted with the painful reality of journals suddenly disappearing from a service. This has been happening for years, of course, on some of the aggregator services for more popular titles, but it is a relatively new phenomenon for publisher-hosted Web sites. If a library has gone to electronic subscriptions, it may suddenly be without any recourse for access.

In Elsevier's case, there have been journals that were available on ScienceDirect but are not presently offered there. While the archiving policy covers this possibility, that does not make it any more acceptable to a library whose access suddenly disappears. What we are to do is: (1) to avoid this happening in the future and (2) to contact the current publishers of the journals taken off ScienceDirect to see if we can license non-exclusive rights to the volumes we published, to be accessed only by existing subscribers. In addition, we have taken this issue to the International Association of Scientific, Technical and Medical Publishers (STM) to seek industry agreement on reciprocal non-exclusive rights when journals change hands.

Interlibrary Loan

When publishers first started offering electronic versions of journals that were also in paper, the tendency was to not permit the use of the electronic copies as a source for interlibrary loan. The assumption was the library had the paper copy and could use it. Almost from the beginning, though, libraries began to assert their need for ILL from the electronic files. Arguments made about improved efficiency had only limited impact on publishers–was it really in the publisher's interest to have efficient ILL? But the arguments soon came to focus on what happens in an e-only world: would libraries not be allowed to do interlibrary loan? Publishers believe that as the penetration of electronic services increases, there will be less and less need for ILL (or document delivery). But, *less* does not equal *no* need. Therefore, there was a requirement that some provision be made for using electronic files for ILL. Elsevier and now several other publishers have accepted this need and make provision in their licenses for the terms under which e-files can be used to support ILL.

Electronic Backfiles

Elsevier Science and some other publishers, such as the American Physical Society and the American Chemical Society, have announced their intention to digitize their backfiles. When this happens, it will increase the opportunity for libraries to free up shelf space, making it more natural to move from paper + electronic to electronic-only.

Divergence of Paper and Electronic

One of the concerns about paper is that it will increasingly be different from–less than–the electronic journals. While the expected great discrepancies in content have not (yet) occurred–there is still relatively little video, audio, animation, large appended data sets, etc.–the growth in linking, when added to desktop availability and searching, makes electronic journals increasingly the medium of choice. The publisher's CrossRef initiative permits linking among the journals of more than 65 publishers.[8] For the user, it is less whether the scientific content in the paper version is complete–it normally is–but rather what you can do with the article once you are there. Links to cited references and, in the near future, forward linking to articles citing the base article will enhance navigation. The same is true with the "more like this" or "more from this author" commands. The electronic environment should be expected to increase the push for e-only access.

Timing of Publication

When we and other publishers first started making journals available electronically, we did it by scanning the printed issue. That meant the electronic version was inherently late. This was an understandable disappointment for those librarians looking to electronic delivery to provide faster delivery. Next came parallel electronic and paper publication–release of the electronic file at the same time as the journal was going on press or into the mails. Today, within ScienceDirect the electronic issue is available at or ahead of the paper more than 95% of the time. But publishers can do better and as an industry they are increasingly releasing articles as soon as they are ready for publication.

In these cases publishers may not wait for the assignment of an issue, volume or page number. The article will be posted online when it has been refereed, accepted and made ready for publication. This, as with linking and electronic enhancements, will drive the push to subscribe to electronic versions, if not e-only.

Electronic Access to "Non-Subscribed Titles" (Titles for Which There Is No Paper Subscription)

Several publishers offer libraries an opportunity to get access in electronic form to titles not currently subscribed to in paper. This may be through the purchase of an electronic subscription to the entire collection or transactional pay-per-view access. Elsevier offers both, including specialized subject collections, where you can supplement your paper + electronic subscriptions with a package of e-only subscriptions to related titles in the same discipline, at a significantly reduced price. Within consortia there can be a variation on this theme, with all libraries having access to anything at least one member subscribes to, often at a very small additional charge.

All of these are variants on the all paper + electronic or all electronic-only themes. Some libraries will maintain a core collection in both paper and electronic forms and have more peripheral titles with only electronic access. What is happening is the broadening of the amount of material available for immediate, desktop access.

In this environment, it could be argued that while the brand name of the journal remains important for authors and readers, the article becomes more and more the unit of interaction. Electronic access has a matrix quality–browse by journal issue or search across the whole database for specific items of interest. From the usage figures already available, it is clear that there are many articles of value to readers in the electronic-only, previously not-subscribed-to titles. This pattern, if it persists, may strengthen the acceptability of electronic-only offerings, as the use of such information has an equal or near equal value to use from subscribed (in paper) titles.

Pricing of Electronic-Only

For the moment, the pricing of most electronic versions of journals is tied to the print subscription price. Receiving only the electronic files usually results either in the same price as the paper or a discount off either the print price alone or the combined print + electronic price.

It can be expected that electronic pricing will ultimately move much more toward some form of usage-based pricing. Some publishers now offer a model that ties to the number of simultaneous users. What the configuration(s) will be in the future remains to be determined, although the preference is likely to be for fixed-price annual subscriptions that have a relationship to the size of the community and level of use, with monitoring of actual use and periodic adjustments up or down. As with the article-level emphasis within a database, the new pricing models will more easily support electronic-only purchases.

The End of Print: Author Concerns

Some of the predictions about the future are suggested above: the community has embraced electronic versions of journals for their availability, speed of release and enhanced functionality. Just as electronic publishing of secondary services came to overtake paper, causing cancellations and electronic-only access for most institutions, so too is the movement to e-only there for many institutional subscribers. The question is: when will publishers stop printing paper? Most publishers are unwilling to make any predictions on that topic. It is not just a question of when the university and research library community worldwide will be ready for electronic-only. It is also when editors and authors will be ready for there to be no paper versions of the journal.

Many publishers have experienced problems getting sufficient submissions for e-only journals–problems to the point of failure of the journal. Authors are concerned about visibility of their articles (something that is much more advantageous with electronic distribution) but they are also concerned about reliable, permanent archiving and access to their articles. They are not writing just for today's readers (those who would be able to access the article if it was "self-archived" on the author's computer or the author's institutional server), but for the researcher of the next decade or century. That access has traditionally been provided by paper journals in libraries. Until the author is assured that a system is in place to do this for electronic journals, paper will continue to be required.

CONCLUSION

We are just beginning to gain experience with the replacement of paper subscriptions with electronic versions. Individual scientists have been the early adopters with respect to society-offered publications. While there has been some hesitation within corporate libraries, given their non-archival role they can be expected to switch soon, as the value of the electronic versions becomes more and more compelling to corporate researchers. The addition of backfiles will hasten the acceptance of electronic-only. But the critical pieces will be the assurance of reliable electronic archiving and, perhaps to a lesser degree, the resolution of government discrimination against electronic products in library funding and taxation. When these issues are resolved to the satisfaction of all stakeholders, the permanent decision to "stop the presses" may be close at hand.

REFERENCES

1. Private communication of 2/4/01 from Tim Ingoldsby, American Institute of Physics.

2. Ingoldsby.

3. Private communication of 2/5/01 from Tom McIlrath, American Physical Society.

4. From a paper, *The Transition from Print to Electronic Journals: A Case Study*, sent to me by its author, Neil McLean (mclean@library.mq.edu.au).

5. Private communication of 1/10/01 from Peter King, University of Bristol.

6. McLean.

7. Private communication of 2/9/01 from Kari Stange, BIBSAM (The Swedish Royal Library's Department for National Co-ordination and Development), with comments from Jan Hagerlid, Swedish University of Agricultural Sciences, Terje Höiseth, Luleå University of Technology, Eva Hesselgren Mortensen, Karlstad University and Kari Stange on behalf of BIBSAM as consortium administrator.

8. See <http://www.crossref.org> for further information.

Songs of the Dodo:
Information Extinctions, Innovation,
and Ecosystem Change

Dennis Dillon

The last man to see a living dodo was Volquard Iverson in 1662. The dodo did not leave much in the way of archives. We have no fossils, no preserved eggs, no stuffed or preserved specimens. We do have a handful of written records, a few paintings, a dried foot, and three or four pieced together partial skeletons. The one complete specimen was held in the Ashmolean Museum at Oxford University. This stuffed unfortunate was consigned to the flames in 1755 by the order of the museum directors. A rebellious curator did manage to save a foot and skull. If the dodo had a song, no one ever bothered to make note of it.

The dodo's environment changed dramatically in 1598 when the Dutchman, Jacob Cornelius introduced non-native livestock into Mauritius and promoted the dodo as a source of wild meat for Dutch sailors. The dodo was never able to adapt, and was extinct within 60 years.

Environmental change has also played a part in the extinction of certain types of communication technology. The last Egyptian hieroglyph was written on August 24th, 394. Neither the Greeks nor the Romans understood hieroglyphic writing, even though it had existed for over 3,000 years. With the discovery of the Rosetta stone in 1799, scholars were able to decipher hieroglyphs from the Egyptian classical period, but early hieroglyphic writing remains a mystery.

Dennis Dillion is Head, Collections & Information Resources, University of Texas at Austin.

[Haworth co-indexing entry note]: "Songs of the Dodo: Information Extinctions, Innovation, and Ecosystem Change." Dillon, Dennis. Co-published simultaneously in *Journal of Library Administration* (The Haworth Information Press, an imprint of The Haworth Press, Inc.) Vol. 35, No. 3, 2001, pp. 67-78; and: *Impact of Digital Technology on Library Collections and Resource Sharing* (ed: Sul H. Lee) The Haworth Information Press, an imprint of The Haworth Press, Inc., 2001, pp. 67-78. Single or multiple copies of this article are available for a fee from The Haworth Document Delivery Service [1-800-HAWORTH, 9:00 a.m. - 5:00 p.m. (EST). E-mail address: getinfo@haworthpressinc.com].

While Egypt eventually evolved a hieroglyphic script that could be used on papyrus, her neighbors invented a new simpler system of communication, the phonetic alphabet. Egypt resisted the new alphabetic technology until the second and third centuries A.D. By 395, the Egyptian hieroglyph was no longer a living means of communication.

What causes extinction? Environmental change is a major culprit. Few organisms, for example, are able to survive an ice age. The dodos were unable to survive the insertion of humankind into their environment. The Egyptians' isolated and rare writing system was unable to survive continual competition from the technologically superior writing systems used by their neighbors.

What does this have to do with libraries? The environment in which libraries operate is also changing. Will the printed book survive? Will the traditional library become extinct? Will future library directors consign the last printed book to the same flames that consumed the Oxford dodo? By using the tools of the life sciences to examine the changes occurring within the ecological system of libraries, publishing, and scholarly communication, we can gain additional insight into the challenges facing all of us.

For example if we consider the printed book as an information species, we can then use these analytical tools to estimate the book's chances for survival or extinction. We can study where the printed book's ecological niche overlaps with the niche of the World Wide Web, where the printed book's niche overlaps (or not) with that of the e-book, how its niche differs from that of the journal article, and so forth and so on. Likewise, we could shift our focus to another level of granularity and treat the library as an information species, asking questions such as: how secure is the library in its present niche, and will the library be able to adapt as its habitat and competitors change?

At one level this is silliness. Human institutions and technological diffusion are not subject to the same influences and constraints as living species. Let's turn our attention to firmer ground, to something that lies at the heart of our traditional understanding of the library–the printed book.

The preacher in Ecclesiastes noted that "of the making of many books there is no end."[1] Closer to our own time a commentator observed, "Trees go to the pulp mills every day, paper gets made, presses roll constantly, and we bob along on a flood of printed words, a great tepid and oily deluge of discourse, nearly all of which is as dispensable as sewage."[2] Here we have two similar viewpoints from both before and after Gutenberg.

Yet, there has always been something special about the book. In the war between chaos and order, between form and formlessness, the book represents a confidence that the world is knowable. That life itself can be cataloged and recorded, that our thoughts and observations can be preserved. That knowledge can be shared between men of different lands and languages, across generations and cultural divides. The book suggests that communication on matters of supreme importance is not only possible, but that it can be conducted with a certain assurance, confirmed by both the legacies of history and by the book's enduring physical existence. Now technology has called this assurance into question. Who among us can trust that the arrangement of magnetic forces on a computer hard drive, or that the ghostly optical transformations on a CD-ROM, will possess any meaning for our children ten generations removed in a world we cannot imagine?

We preside in an age of unparalleled libraries and archives, yet this is also an age that has loosed phantom changelings into a previously stable information environment. The bulk of humanity's communication during the twentieth century has been dribbled away on the will o'wisp electron–radio and television broadcasts, web pages, communications carried on electromagnetic mediums of every kind–all gone as if they had never happened. A continual babble of human discourse, overwhelming in its magnitude and variety, as irretrievably gone as the song of the dodo, as lost to future human interpretation as the early Egyptian hieroglyphics. Yet, as librarians we know that we cannot save every word and utterance, and as consumers, we know that not everything is worth saving.

Loss, decay, deterioration, extinction–these are all nature's way of taking out the trash, nature's way of opening up space for innovation and adaptation.

And while electronic communication does not enjoy the inherent permanence of words carved in stone, or even of ink on paper, who can deny the obvious benefits of the electrified and networked world? Whether sending moving pictures through the air, or e-mail through optical cables, all of these innovations have had the effect of bringing humankind closer together. Given the many changes in the information environment however, one can't help but wonder if libraries and books as we know them will survive another century. Even a hundred years ago in Victorian England, Alice asked in the opening paragraph of *Alice in Wonderland,* "What's the use of a book without pictures or conversation?"[3]

THE CALVARIA TREE

In 1977 an ecologist named Stanley Temple published an article in Science magazine revealing that there were only thirteen old and dying Calvaria trees remaining on the island of Mauritius. The seeds of the current trees weren't germinating, and as near as he could tell, they hadn't germinated for hundreds of years. Because the Calvaria had evolved extremely thick-walled seed pits, the seeds were unable to germinate unless they were first abraded and scarified by the gizzard of the dodo.[4] Stephen Jay Gould expanded upon this discovery in Natural History magazine, and it was recounted in the London Times and other newspapers, eventually becoming one of the standard textbook examples of mutualism and the cascading ramifications of extinction. Unfortunately, it's also a textbook example of the quickness of today's publication cycles, and the dangers of hit and run science. Biologists in Mauritius and neighboring islands chuckled at the gullibility of the outside experts. In actuality there are hundreds of Calvaria trees that have germinated since the extinction of the dodo.[5] Stanley Temple just didn't know where to look, and he let his preconceived assumptions get in the way of studying a situation that was more complex than he had imagined.

ADAPTATION

Evolution proceeds through adaptation to the local environment. In the case of the Calvaria tree, it turns out that fruit bats and parrots also help to scatter and break down the tree's seeds. In the history of communication, we have also seen continual adaptation and innovation–from stone carving, to clay tablets, to the Internet.

And just like the Calvaria tree, information seldom stands alone. It exists within an ecological system that includes highly evolved methods of organization, distribution, and access.

Among the more enduring adaptations in information handling was the idea of putting things in alphabetical order which began during the 1780s, and the adoption of the filing cabinet in the 1890s. Both of these innovations spread throughout the world quickly to every office and institution that handled information. Like the World Wide Web, both systems resulted in quicker, more convenient access to information and both systems reduced the amount of specialized elite knowledge a user needed in order to access information.[6]

These concepts resurfaced in the thinking of scientists at Xerox PARC in the 1970s where they emerged as the personal computer with its familiar graphical user interface of digital documents, files, folders, and alphabetical menus which could be navigated by pointing, clicking, and scrolling.

However, the Xerox development engineers in Dallas found the scientists arrogant and unintelligible. Management found them naïve and unrealistic. And the scientist regarded the other groups as "toner heads" unable to imagine a world beyond photocopiers.[7] As a consequence it took a different company, Apple Computer, to license these discoveries and pioneer the modern computer as we know it. Xerox had become over-specialized and ecologically isolated from the wider environment. The company was unable to adapt as the environment around them changed.

EXTINCTION

In a pioneering 1983 paper entitled "What do we really know about extinction?" Michael Soule mentioned four acknowledged causes of extinction: habitat destruction, ecological isolation, competition, and predation.[8] Libraries have reason to pay attention to each of these four threats.

Habitat Destruction. While there has never been as much information as there is now, the habitat that libraries occupy is that of middleman between information producer and information consumers. A significant reason for the existence of libraries, in the eyes of their funding institutions, lies in the efficiencies of scale, convenience, and cost savings that libraries have been able to provide when compared to existing alternatives. This habitat is now under threat.

Ecological Isolation. Libraries are wholly dependent on a single source of nourishment, that of their parent funding organization. In this sense they are ecologically isolated and perpetually at risk.

Competition. The Internet brings a wealth of instantly accessible information to anyone with an Internet connected computer. Like Egyptian hieroglyphs facing the threat of the phonetic alphabet, libraries face a threat from a quicker, easier, and potentially more universal means of information access.

Predation. Predation can come in many forms. As Will Cuppy noted in his several 1940s instruction manuals on how to become extinct: "The last two Great Auks (Northern Penguins) in the world were killed June 4th, 1844 on the island of Eldey, off the coast of Iceland . . . I'm afraid the Great Auks were pretty foolish . . . Like dodos, they had a tendency to pal with just anybody. Whenever they noticed someone creeping up on them with a blunt instrument, they would rush to meet him with glad little squawks of welcome and stick out their necks. Both species did this once too often."[9] As our parents always told us, sometimes your choice of friends can get you into a lot of trouble.

PROGRESS

Extinction of one species opens up an ecological niche for a new species. The definition of an ecological niche is the set of resources, physical conditions, and behavioral possibilities within which a population of organisms lives. Every species must have its own niche.

If we treated journals as an information species and applied this definition, we would say that no two journals can occupy the same niche. Eventually one of them must shift its subject focus, its price, its method of delivery, its audience, its format, etc.–so that it does not occupy the same niche as its competitor. This is part of the thinking behind SPARC, in which competitive journals have been established to occupy the same niche (except for price) as an existing journal.[10]

Books are an entirely different breed of information species. Unlike issues of a journal, every book stands alone and must make its own way in the world. Books do not reap benefits from being sold via subscriptions like journals, nor do books benefit from the referrals that journals receive from indexing and abstracting services. The niche for books is very different from that of journals. However, the niche for both printed books and journals has been relatively stable until recently. In contrast, the niches occupied by e-books, e-journals, and other electronic information bit streams continue to evolve rapidly. It would be very surprising if remnants of the arbitrary distinctions that e-this, e-that, and e-everything else brought with them over from the print world, last long in the new electronic environment

As we all know from the millennium dot.com meltdown, technological niches are sensitive to a whole host of influences. For example, in 1947 RCA was marketing a fax machine called the Ultrafax that could fax an entire book across the country in less than a minute. However RCA soon discovered that no one wanted to send books across the country in a minute and the product failed.[11] The culture was not ready for this particular innovation. There was no environmental need for instant communication of this type in 1947. The appropriate niche for it did not yet exist.

Ever since the Enlightenment, western civilization has believed in the concept of progress: intelligent use of technology leads to material progress, which in turn leads to general social and cultural progress . . . and so the wheel turns. We find it comforting to believe that everyday, in everyway, we are getting better and better. Here's another view of progress and adaptation. The Old Testament is full of accounts of chariots and carts, and yet two thousand years later wheels had virtually disappeared as a means of transportation throughout thousands of miles of Biblical civilization. They were replaced by the camel. Camels could ford rivers, traverse rough ground, and required less staff to manage than a wagon.[12] From the perspective of technological progress, this switch from the wheel to the camel was a step backward, but from an evolutionary perspective, this was another case of adaptation to the local environment. Wheels work well for certain purposes, camels work better for others. In our own field this has echoes in the ongoing print versus digital discussion.

On my campus some people believe that print is doomed, and that digital information is as inevitable as a divine bolt of lightening dispensed by Zeus himself. Others do not believe that the situation is this simple. If we are to believe the lessons of the life sciences, no technology is inevitable. Technology adapts to environmental niches: to the set of resources, physical conditions, and behavioral possibilities in which a population lives.

TECHNOLOGICAL INNOVATION

In my own library we have been canceling print journals in favor of their e-journal clones. Just a few years ago we didn't even have any e-journals. In searching the literature for an explanation of how this rapid change in affairs came to pass, I found an explanation in an apocryphal Texas tale about the discovery and creation of pickups. Supposedly, a group of west Texas cowboys were trying to move a large boulder and succeeded in getting it rolling downhill, whereupon it picked up speed and landed on the back of the ranch owner's new sedan squashing the tail portion, but leaving the front seat untouched. Being cheap, the owner continued to drive the vehicle and began using the squashed back to carry things that wouldn't fit in the front seat. Other cowboys saw this, and consumed by envy, began dropping boulders on their own sedans copycat fashion, and thus the pickup was born. This tale of local adaptation to an existing environmental niche, also illustrates the process of technological diffusion, and to a certain degree explains what has happened with journals.

If we envision technological innovation as the boulder that rolled down the hill and landed square atop the print journal squashing it flat, then the resulting Texas pickup is the e-journal. Just as the cowboys all wanted the new pickup, libraries wanted the new e-journals. E-journals provided utility that could not be found in the print journal.

Now it's likely that if a beam fell off a skyscraper and landed on a sedan in New York City that the city dweller would not react like the Texas ranch owner. It's unlikely that New Yorkers would see the added utility that could come from squashing their cars with falling beams–which just goes to show that Texas ranchers live in a different niche than New Yorkers–and that we cannot expect everyone to be equally open to technological and cultural change. In other words, circumstances have to be just right for innovation to be accepted.

CONTEXT

The squashed car in Texas exists within a different context than the squashed car in New York. Context is important. Andre Gide once said "Fish die belly upward and rise to the surface; it is their way of falling."[13] That's context. Or if you prefer an illustration from baseball, Dave Barry noted with sorrow that, "If a woman has to choose between catching a fly ball and saving an infant's life, she will choose to save the infant's life, without even considering that there are men on base."[14] That's a conflict in context. With a book, its context is not obvious until you finish reading and put it down, and even then my context may be different from yours. This is relative context. When dealing with information and innovation, the importance of context cannot be overemphasized.

Knowledge and existing beliefs form the scaffolding that allows us to evaluate new ideas. Context allows us to find a place to hang our new ideas. In our current thinking, we tend to place e-books within the context of printed books, though as intellectual property rendered in an electromagnetic medium, they could just as easily be mentally pigeonholed beside syndicated radio broadcasts, scrambled satellite transmissions, or your mother's web site.

How can libraries adapt and survive in a shifting environment in which newly hatched information mutants such as e-books flit about without a properly understood context?

As librarians, one of the things we do is make selections between options. In this role we are constantly making choices. We decide to keep the print. Or we go digital. Or we answer a user's question, or we don't. These are all choices that affect both our profession and who we will be in the future. Every library is the result of countless tradeoffs and compromises. That is what makes it a collection. Many minds, many opinions go into its making. And it is the totality of the collection that provides our users with context. The key to making the collection a success is responsible judgment. As Noam Chomsky has noted, "As soon as questions of will or decision or reason or choice of action arise, human science is at a loss."[15] What takes over then is professional knowledge: the intelligence that we have painfully gleaned from our working environment and the publishing ecosystem, what we know of our library, and the professional competencies and confidences that we have accrued throughout a lifetime of hard won wisdom.

How then can libraries best withstand the vagaries of environmental change? Context is part of the answer. Learning occurs when new ideas are associated and connected with previous knowledge, when new ideas can be affixed to the scaffolding provided by reliable context. If library users can count on the integrity of the scaffolding accessible through the library, count on the context provided through library efforts, then they have found firm ground that they cannot easily find elsewhere. Librarians are uniquely positioned to be a source of this scaffolding, to be a source of reliable context uncolored by commercial interests or personal gain. So this is part of the answer–librarians of integrity and judgment, providing their users with a reliable framework in which to pursue their interests.

THE INTERNET

So where are we? Let's return to *Alice in Wonderland* where we now find that Alice has been joined by the dodo. Alice and her friends have become thoroughly soaked and they are arguing about how to dry out. Finally the dodo can stand it no longer and offers a suggestion. "The best thing to get us dry," says the dodo, "would be a Caucus-race." The dodo then lays out a circular course and places everyone at random starting points. They all begin running when they like and leave off when they like, and it is easy to know when the race is over. But once they had been running awhile and were quite dry the dodo suddenly called out "The race is over!" The participants were puzzled and asked "But who has won?" This was a question the dodo could not answer and he remained deep in thought for some time. Finally the dodo said "Everybody has won and all must have prizes."[16] So what happened in this tale is that the dodo took a group that was all wet and got them to work together to achieve a higher purpose (getting dry) and then gave them all prizes for cooperating and achieving their higher ends. The lesson is that it does not matter who wins the race, if everyone's ends are achieved and all are rewarded.

We all know that the Web enables new ways of approaching traditional task and functions. For example: *gainsharing* in which innovative uses of technology allow both parties to gain. In our industry, this can take the form of a publisher locking in current revenue via a multi-year contract, and in return granting a consortia access to a greater wealth of content. Both parties benefit from this arrangement, at least in the short term. *Disintermediation,* which allows a student to use an e-journal and e-book without having to go to the library. *Dematerialization,* in which businesses shift from a strategy of ownership to leasing, whether it be buildings, vehicles, or information–thereby reducing overhead costs as well as commitment to any particular solution set. All of these examples of Internet economics, can be viewed as potential win-win situations, in which all parties benefit through the efficiencies and new business models enabled by the World Wide Web.

It may be that the Web, by opening up new ways of thinking about old problems, is a modern form of the Caucus-race, with no beginning and no end, where the best institutional strategy is to follow the advice of the dodo, and to use the potential of the Web to make everyone a winner.

BRICOLAGE

However, John Seeley Brown, the chief scientist at Xerox PARC, argues that the tools of the academy–deductive and abstract classical reasoning–are not well suited to the Web environment. He suggests that bricolage, the ability to look around one's self, use one's creative judgment, and find the appropriate objects needed in order to build something, are skills more appropriate to the Web.[17]

The form of reasoning known as bricolage was first elaborated in the early 1960s by Claude Levi Strauss and was born out of observing the learning habits of young children.[18] Bricolage does not assume that the ends are clearly known before a process begins, and it does not use logical reasoning to achieve its ends, but tends to employ more of a creative tinkering process. This entire paper was constructed as an exercise in bricolage, an assemblage of disparate facts into a whole that may or may not illuminate the topic under discussion. If the hypertext environment of the Web invites the use of thinking skills other than the Western deductive approaches that some claim are an outgrowth of our peculiar linear alphabetic technology,[19] then our information ecology may be in for even more changes than we have previously suspected.

SUMMARY

So, what is the postcard version of the discussion in this paper? That it is useful to look at our present situation from the perspective of an ecology of information, because the Web has radically altered the information environment and our potential courses of action. New information species and niches are evolving rapidly. That tools developed to understand the constantly evolving complexity of living organisms can provide a useful framework from which to understand an information environment that is no longer relatively linear and static, but complex, evolving, and unpredictable.

If you recall, we began our discussion with the dodo, and have journeyed through extinction, biology, technology, the printed book, libraries, Egypt, pickup trucks, the social sciences, the history of the camel and the wheel, the alphabet, baseball, *Alice in Wonderland*, Internet economics, the Bible, Xerox PARC, and Claude Levis Strauss–so where does this exercise end? It ends with fishing. John Buchan, the famous Scottish author and statesman, said "The charm of fishing is that it is the pursuit of what is elusive but attainable, a perpetual series of occasions for hope."[20] That is what librarianship is today, an elusive but attainable, perpetual series of occasions for hope.

REFERENCES

1. Bible. Old Testament. Ecclesiastes, 12:12.
2. Quammen on Pulp Mills–Wild Thoughts p. 219.
3. Lewis Carroll, "The Annotated Alice: Alice's Adventures in Wonderland & Through the Looking Glass, with introduction and notes by Martin Gardner, (New York, Clarkson N. Potter, 1960), 25.
4. Stanley Temple, "Plant-animal mutualism: coevolution with dodo leads to near extinction of plant," Science (August 2, 1977), 885-6.

5. David Quammen, Song of Dodo (London, Pimlico,1996), 347-352.

6. Edward Tenner, "From Slip to Chip," Harvard Magazine (November/December 1990), 52-57.

7. John Seely Brown and Paul Duguid, The Social Life of Information (Boston: Harvard Business School Press, 2000), 150.

8. Michael Soule, "What do we really know about extinction?" in Christine Schonewald-Cox, ed., Genetics and Conservation (Menlo Park, CA: Benjamin/ Cummings, 1983).

9. Will Cuppy, The Great Bustard and Other People, quoted in Dena Jones Jolma, Hunting Quotations: two hundred years of writings on the philosophy, culture, and experience (Jefferson, N.C.: McFarland, 1992), 100.

10. Scholarly Publishing and Academic Resources Coalition. <http://www.arl.org/sparc/home>.

11. Maurice Fabre, The History of Communication (NY: Hawthorne Books, 1963), 97.

12. Richard W. Bulliet, The Camel and the Wheel (Cambridge, Mass.: Harvard University Press, 1975).

13. Andrew Gide quoted in, 21st Century Dictionary of Quotations (New York: Dell, 1993).

14. Dave Barry quoted in "Sports Quotes," URL: <http://www.geocities.com/ SouthBeach/Marina/9676/sportsq.html>.

15. Noam Chomsky quoted in The Oxford Dictionary of Quotations (Oxford: Oxford University Press, 1996), 200.

16. Lewis Carroll, "The Annotated Alice: Alice's Adventures in Wonderland & Through the Looking Glass, with introduction and notes by Martin Gardner, (New York, Clarkson N. Potter, 1960), 48-49.

17. John Seely Brown, "Growing up Digital: How the Web Changes Work, Education, and the Ways People Learn." Change (March/April 200),11-20.

18. Claude Levi-Strauss, The Savage Mind (Chicago, The University of Chicago Press, 1996), 16-36.

19. Robert K. Logan, The Alphabet Effect: The impact of the phonetic alphabet on the development of western civilization (New York: William Morrow, 1986), 20-21.

20. John Buchan quoted in Edward Murphy, The Crown Treasury of Relevant Quotations, (New York, Crown Publishers, 1978).

Special Collections Libraries
in the Digital Age:
A Scholarly Perspective

Charles T. Cullen

Several years ago at another conference sponsored by the University of Oklahoma Libraries, a very good presentation on the future of research posited a fanciful future scene of a scholar with access through a personal computer to everything necessary to write a focused study of an author and her work. What could make this possible was the Internet and all its possibilities, at that time only just coming into its own. Familiarity among scholars with html and Web sites and hyperlinks was not yet widespread, although the possibilities and probabilities were promising much that raised excitement and created expectations. The assumption then, if not now, was that everything would become available on the Web, and the methods and practices of scholarly research would change dramatically and forever. The speaker at that conference imagined all of this in place by 2003.[1] While futurists assumed it would happen, it was yet so early in the transition that little discussion was being held about how it should or would happen. It seemed so easy to scan texts and convert objects into digital form, and scholars were beginning to discover that digitization could in some instances enhance one's ability to get information from some texts that in manuscript had heretofore been impossible or exceedingly difficult to read. Why would the hold-

Charles T. Cullen is President and Librarian, The Newberry Library.

[Haworth co-indexing entry note]: "Special Collections Libraries in the Digital Age: A Scholarly Perspective." Cullen, Charles T. Co-published simultaneously in *Journal of Library Administration* (The Haworth Information Press, an imprint of The Haworth Press, Inc.) Vol. 35, No. 3, 2001, pp. 79-91; and: *Impact of Digital Technology on Library Collections and Resource Sharing* (ed: Sul H. Lee) The Haworth Information Press, an imprint of The Haworth Press, Inc., 2001, pp. 79-91. Single or multiple copies of this article are available for a fee from The Haworth Document Delivery Service [1-800-HAWORTH, 9:00 a.m. - 5:00 p.m. (EST). E-mail address: getinfo@haworthpressinc.com].

79

ers of rich and potentially rich collections NOT digitize their holdings and make them available widely on the Internet? It was then, and it still is, an exciting time in which to be working on such issues.

At the outset I should make it clear that I favor converting all our special collections and much, if not all, of our regular holdings into full digital format–images of all objects and digital text conversion to allow for searching for any manner of word or combination of words. Indeed, with advanced programming, it ought to be possible to search for concepts as well as specific alphanumeric characters. Why would anyone argue that this would not be ideal for the student and the scholar, or for anyone? Like free tuition for all it would be a wonderful and democratic thing. But like free tuition for all, I recognize that it is not likely to happen, at least not anytime soon. Furthermore, it is a given, I believe, that research materials are going to be digitized to some extent and in some fashion. But the ways in which we have increased access to research materials in the past ought to teach us a good deal about how to go about using the newest technology to transform access. I have in mind the work done to prepare microfilm collections of research materials and the monumental labor of the second half of the last century to prepare comprehensive editions of the writings of many people and some thematic studies whose collections help illuminate our past.

When work began in mid-century on editing the letters and papers of Thomas Jefferson and other notables who had left behind large collections, increasing access to accurate texts was the primary motivation. It was thought that publishing these texts in authoritative and comprehensive form would enable worldwide dissemination. No longer would scholars seeking the information in these documents have to travel to several, and in some cases, many repositories to read and learn from these sources. Even the average citizen interested in the history of our nation would have easy access in this printed form. Jefferson himself had made the argument when he wrote in 1791, "... let us save [historic documents]: not by vaults and locks which fence them from the public eye and use . . . but by such a multiplication of copies, as shall place them beyond the reach of accident."[2] This project departed from the standard practice of earlier editions of papers of famous people, whereby only the texts (and only selected texts) of the subject were transcribed and printed. The designer of the new Jefferson edition broke with tradition and established a new standard by adopting a policy of including both outgoing and incoming correspondence, in order to provide the complete context of the papers and as complete as possible source material to help readers understand what they were reading. This was at the time revolutionary, and it changed forever the way in which documentary editing would be done. Following on the heels of this project was the establishment of other similar projects, notably one at the Massachusetts Historical Society to publish the entire span of papers of the Adams Family from John and Abigail through Henry, more than a century of family papers. Recognizing the length of time the undertaking would require and the attendant delay in providing access to the full collection, the editors of this project decided to prepare a microfilm edition of the papers at the start of their work. This also was a revolutionary approach to the preparation of a collection of primary materials for widespread dissemination. Traditionally, collections of documents were disseminated in microfilm or printed form, but seldom in both formats. Because microfilm readers had become more widespread after World War II and scholars had relatively easy access to them in libraries, a 100+ reel set of film containing all of the Adams Family Papers made good sense at the outset of preparation of an edition that would take perhaps a century to prepare in letterpress format.

My point in these examples is simple. New ideas and new methods of access led to decisions that, once made, had significant repercussions. By the late 1960s, almost 50 projects had embarked on editorial projects to prepare scholarly editions of the papers of many American figures from the Revolution to the present. Improving access was the primary objective, with spreading the sources of democracy being the chief secondary motive and what produced a couple of million dollars annually from Congress to be used in the work. It was, after all, the era of the Cold War. Democratizing access was a corollary, as well.

My point in these examples also relates to the impact of new ideas and technology on the dissemination of resource materials. Before these editions could be brought close to completion, changes in technology introduced new and better methods of improving access to this information that far exceed the wildest imaginations of those who started the work not so long ago. Who would launch a project today to prepare an important collection of materials without plans for putting it on the Internet? Indeed, the chief financial backer of these many editions, the National Historical Publications and Records Commission, requires an electronic component in all new proposals. And who would think that an enterprise had to be established at a fixed site where copies of all the papers would be assembled and all the work of preparing an edition would of necessity take place? Large caches of Jefferson's papers reside at the Library of Congress, the Massachusetts Historical Society, and the University of Virginia, with significant holdings at many other repositories and in private hands around the world. Before serious work of editing these papers could begin, copies of everything had to be made and assembled, catalogued, and arranged in the editorial offices at Princeton where the scholars would work on them together as they prepared each volume in chronological order. It sounds rather primitive, today.

When I listened at the earlier conference several years ago, I thought of the many different kinds of research and the different kinds of researchers I was familiar with as a scholar and historian. The Jefferson volumes are designed to be used both by the serious scholar and the interested general reader, following a one-for-all editorial policy. Libraries cannot function as simply, especially when they try to deal with the question of what they ought to make available in digital format. In my thinking about collections issues and audiences (users), I distinguish between academic libraries and special collections libraries in the following way: the former have as their primary audience students who are being educated, while the latter have as their primary audience scholars who are creating new scholarship. The one is built around a collection of secondary sources, and the other gathers collections of primary sources. The impact of the new technology is different for each of these, especially if we agree that we do not live in an ideal world and not everything is likely to be digitized.

It is a disturbing trend that finds students conducting research on the Internet without exercising, or knowing how to exercise, judgment about what is reliable and what is not. The new technology, as we all know too well, allows anyone to put up anything without vetting of any kind. It is by no means a given that, if one finds a book in a reputable university library, it is a reputable source. How have we managed to convey to students that some of our holdings contain better scholarship than others? When an upper level undergraduate writes a research paper, how does he or she manage to avoid the poor resources? Of course, they aren't always avoided, but by and large students learn to form judgments about printed and manuscript sources that may not be happening on the Internet in quite the same manner. It may not be happening because today students approach serious research already conditioned to think that they can find anything on the Internet, and if it is there it may to some degree be relied upon. This is particularly dangerous, it seems to me, for secondary sources, but not exclusively. Perhaps it is less easy for a student to know that a text on the Internet is quite an old and out-dated source if, for example, it is a digital version of a book published long ago. If a search engine is used by one interested in the period of the Civil War in Georgia, for example, one might come directly to a history of the state that was in use in classrooms until 1925, a study that hardly mentions slavery, reflecting the view at the time in Georgia and other southern states that constitutional issues caused the war and the way of life that included slavery was one of the victims of the North's victory. Of course, the same search would produce links to dozens if not hundreds or thousands of other sources that might present a multitude of interpretations and views. How do we teach students how to discern between reliable and unreliable interpretation? It is essential that they recognize that history written by a scholar is one person's spin on events in our past, reflecting one person's understanding written from points of view developed in the context of one person's life. I might be persuaded that making all secondary accounts available on the Web would lead to exposure of bad history as well as recognition of the good. Still, the problem of having too much or too little on the Web remains, and the challenge of what is just right won't go away.

I believe we are on safer ground dealing with the impact of the new technology on primary source materials and reference, which is what my library collects. I return to my earlier statement: we should digitize it all. But that simply is not going to happen. I applaud the efforts at several universities where large and important efforts to create digital texts for the use of scholars (and anyone with an Internet connection) are taking place. Scholars have been served very well by the work of some information technologists who have shown them new tools that have enabled them to conduct research that had been impossible before. I have in mind particularly the work with handwritten texts, in my case from the 18th century. Jefferson always drafted his own reports as the nation's first Secretary of State, and he often marked through words as he edited his work. He marked through them in a way that completely obscured them. Digitizing these texts, and applying technology to assign colors to the different inks makes it possible to electronically erase the ink that covers a word to expose the original different ink that lies beneath it. This has made it possible to discern what Jefferson's thought process was as he wrote, and it has also made much clearer in some cases the context of his concerns over the issues at hand. For this and other reasons, the Uva-Monticello-Massachusetts Historical Society edition of Jefferson's *Notes on the State of Virginia* will be better than any of its printed editions and better even than the original, heavily edited manuscript copy used by Jefferson over a period of many years.

While this is, to me, a good example, I hasten to observe that not much of Jefferson's writing has been digitized. And a closer look at the possible digitization of his writings leads us to some points that all of us have to consider as we try to answer questions about the new technology and special collections. In 1999 I learned that one of the old printed editions of Jefferson's writings was now available on the Internet. I was disappointed to learn, however, that what had been put up was the Lipscomb and Berg edition. This was the most flawed edition of the several done before 1950, and it had the added limitation of containing only Jefferson's side of the correspondence, a side that was sometimes edited for reasons known only to Lipscomb and Berg and lacking notes to indicate what had been omitted from a letter. I asked those who had digitized the text why they chose this flawed edition. Their response referred to lack of copyright problems and a recognition that it was a poor edition, but a final declaration that it was better to have this one available than to have nothing there. As a scholar I must disagree. Those who have worked with Jefferson's papers know that one has to read a great deal to discern what he truly thought and believed. It does not become readily apparent by reading a few letters or only one side of the correspondence that he tended to write people what he thought they wanted to hear. To read a beautifully written letter to St. George Tucker on the latter's proposal for the gradual abolition of slavery would lead the casual reader to think Jefferson was passionately opposed to slavery (herein he refers to his fears for the safety of whites if God is just). Having access to Tucker's letter and his proposal helps put Jefferson's remarks in context and, when read with others written in response to the gift of unsolicited pamphlets and proposals, sheds a different light on Jefferson's own writing to these people. The best way to share that insight with others who read his writings is to make them all available with scholarly annotation by the best students of Jefferson studies wherever in the world they may be.

What do we choose to digitize? Selection is an important issue that has been written about quite a lot, and the issues are different as the collections and the potential users of the collections differ. As suggested above, what we might digitize for the use of teaching students in an undergraduate curriculum in the liberal arts is not what we might select for a scholar needing special collections to write new scholarship. What priority do we assign to a conversion project? Should we digitize as a conservation measure, requiring patrons to use the electronic version in order to preserve the original (as the Library of Congress does on microfilm with its Jefferson letters)? Do we digitize materials with the world in mind, or do we focus on special interest users and let others take care of themselves? This might seem to be a distinction without a difference, but I don't think it is. In deciding to undertake any digitization project, special collections librarians need to answer these questions and others as they determine the motivation in doing a certain collection or object in their collections, the design of the project (is the material like Jefferson's edited letters or the *Notes on the State of Virginia* with many emanations and interlineations, or is it straightforward text?), the functionality and purpose of the project, and not the least consideration, the funding of it. One has to consider the audience for the material. Let's take *Notes on the State of Virginia* once again as an example. How large is the potential audience? Some would argue that it is pretty large, but relatively speaking it is actually quite small in numbers. What is the motivation to do it? Those who own the manuscripts that make it up know that it is a highly complex text that was pasted together and then rearranged over time by Jefferson, even as he edited parts of it after it was printed (presumably thinking of issuing a revised edition). No edition, from 1786 to the present, has ever captured the nature of the manuscript, and none other than the first edition can claim to be arranged as Jefferson first intended it to be. So, preparing a modern electronic edition would enable scholars to piece it together as the manuscript was left by Jefferson at his death, enabling scholars then to learn from it all that they might as though they had access to the manuscript reposed in the Massachusetts Historical Society itself. This manuscript might be tackled by scholars as an interesting exercise in design and functionality, one more interesting than many others that might be done from Jefferson's papers, and one for which funding might be found. All of this being the case, therefore, once this specific, rather focused and targeted project were undertaken, the potential beneficiary pool is much larger than merely a significant number of Jefferson scholars.

This is an example of a project that might be obvious to Jefferson scholars, but how do we decide on other more general interest projects that we might pursue? Surely the kinds of tools we have used in the past may serve to aid us in the future. We know which collections are more heavily used, just as we know which books in our general and special collections are circulated most often. We have used this information to help us make decisions about conservation measures, and even those related to shelving. The computer has emerged as another tool that is very helpful in this regard. But the business people refer to these bits of data as "lagging indicators," telling us about past use. While in our libraries past use is often an indication of future potential use, we might ask ourselves if our computers might be used to provide better future indicators of use in ways not readily seen today. We might be missing something we should know and act upon by looking only at past usage. Indeed, we all know of instances of increased demand and use of material that becomes available in computer form because of the discovery by others that it is available and that it contains useful information. It is that kind of unexpected (and perhaps even consciously unintended) consequence that excites those who have worked to make special materials available in digital form. When the Franklin letters were made available in beta form by the Packard Humanities Institute, several scholars at the Newberry had a great time conducting searches on such words as "Indian" (it turned up hundreds of times) and "nature." One simply cannot do that kind of research with written texts, and doing it with the computer is the surest way to point out the inadequacy of most indexes that appear with printed materials.

In deciding on what to digitize, relying only on past use in a special collections library is wrong or impossible or foolish. We all can cite examples of a book or cache of manuscripts lying unused for decades being taken up by a scholar who sees in them things that had never been seen before, leading to new interpretations and new insights. The Newberry Library's large Renaissance collection has contained items for a century that had never been used until recently by scholars interested in gender studies. Had we chosen to digitize some of it before this work began, and had we consulted lagging indicators of materials used to inform our decisions about what to put on our server, we would have missed much of this, and what we put up might not have been of interest to scholars of gender studies. Although I would quickly agree that one can never predict fully the uses that scholars might make of materials at their disposal, and were we purchasing material based primarily on current scholarly interest, much of what we have might never have made it to our shelves.

As I said earlier, special collections librarians have the opportunity, if not the obligation, to shape their audiences to fit their collections, whereas general collections are more often shaped by their audiences to meet their needs. In the context of the impact of technology on special collections libraries I mean this to say that we should be more proactive in making our resources available to scholars who may not know that they need them. We should be making intelligent decisions about how we can get our materials onto the Web in fully digitized form (image and searchable text), and we should be doing so with all possible haste.

Many of us are putting parts of our collections on the Web, and most of those doing it have developed a plan that fits the work into some overall strategy. Either the collection or items digitized for the Web are outstanding examples from the collection's strengths, or they are excellent items to be used in teaching certain subjects, or they have the potential to excite or illuminate researchers at the same time they bring some degree of glory to the repository for making them so easily and widely available. I have no problem with this, as far as it goes, but it does not go far enough.

If digitizing special collections makes sense, and it surely does, then the technology should be used to make the most sense out of the potential that lies within it. Scholars come to our special collections to use materials we care for. Sometimes it is possible to write a work of scholarship in a single collection, but more often resources from a variety of collections are needed. I can think of no better opportunity for sensible collaboration than the prospect that is now before us. As we think of selecting items to be digitized, it is relatively easy to identify a collection that has been heavily used and that has potential for continued additional use. The Newberry has a collection on the American West, for example, that contains about 10,000 books, and is used by almost all scholars who visit the Newberry to work on topics even remotely related to that field. It is a logical collection to be selected for digitization for many of the same reasons that it was the first of our collections that we chose for retrospective conversion of our catalogue cards. Conversion of the cards has led, as anyone would expect, to increased use of these materials by a wider and more geographically distant audience. As we think of what we ought to do next, we recognize that a related collection is our Edward Ayer collection. This is somewhat more specialized and is one of, if not the, best collection of books and manuscripts on Native Americans. Comprising about 150,000 volumes, a million manuscript pages, 2,000 maps, 500 atlases, 6,000 photographs and 3,500 drawings and paintings on the subject, this collection has been used by scholars to write new interpretations of American history and American Indian culture. It has been used by tribal historians and those studying European culture in the period of exploration of North America. The catalogue records for this collection need conversion, and the entire collection should be digitized.

Converting the catalogue records to computer form is the Newberry's problem and its responsibility. Making digital copies of these materials for widespread use over the Internet is a different matter. Rather than each repository making collections of materials available in digital form to be placed on their own server, it seems to me to make far greater sense for institutions with related materials to collaborate and create digital collections of materials as one (or a few) data bases on one server that itself would become a center for access to these materials in that form. Hyperlinks aside, placing material on several servers with metadata to be found by search engines looking for key words, or even more sophisticated search devices, sets up a kind of cat and mouse game that is perhaps better than nothing, but it is somewhat contrary to the ideal of providing easy access that the computer offers. It can also be somewhat detrimental to scholarship as well.

Slightly more than a decade ago, I had occasion to confer with a dean about his university's special collection library. It was in a building separate from the main library, and its collections were not very much used by faculty or students of his university in spite of its remarkable riches in some areas of the humanities. The dean observed that it was used more by members outside the university (by graduate students and faculty from other universities), and he questioned the high cost of maintaining it without greater use to his own immediate academic community.

This is a sentiment heard less in the 1990s, but it comes to mind when I think of why we have the materials we keep so well and what we should do with them. It comes to mind when we consider whether we should promote their use. The Internet has eliminated many of the boundaries that existed for so long and that enabled us to think of our collections as our own, primarily (if not just) for our own constituency, however broadly or narrowly we defined it. Few of us think we should not make all our catalogue records for our special collections available on the Internet (if indeed all of our special collections are adequately catalogued). Many, if not all, of us most likely agree that providing digital images and texts on the Web is also desirable. Much is being placed there almost daily, and the content is only going to grow over time. Some repositories, like the Library of Congress, may have such deep holdings that they can work toward putting materials online in such a fashion as to be seemingly complete in coverage without collaborating with others. Its American Memory project has seen an impressive quantity and array of primary source material appear on the Web, part of an effort to bring the valuable resources of that institution to more people for their use. I take nothing away from what they are doing and have done, but I would like to think it could be viewed as something greater than one institution's material on one or more subjects. It might be argued that had the Library of Congress designed its huge project as one of collaboration with others with similar and related holdings, it might never have gotten off the ground. That is probably true. I should think few of us consider our collections as providing sufficient coverage of important topics that could be studied without the benefit of related materials at other libraries.

What does the future hold? Surely materials, even entire collections, will continue to be digitized and made available on the Web. Surely, lists of links will appear that will serve as indices to resources of research interests. And Google and other good search programs will lead us to these sources. These kinds of programs will no doubt improve. What I fear, to some extent, is a traffic jam or at least another roadblock in the path of researchers looking for sources. That is what primarily motivates me to suggest that collaboration and joint planning for resource sharing of digital collections is something we should consider. Before the Newberry Library puts large parts (or all) of its Italian Renaissance holdings online, it should confer with the Folger, the Huntington, the Morgan, the British Library, the New York Public Library, the National Library in Florence, and many others to explore the possibility of establishing an online center for all these materials. Each could contribute files to the server, and the digital library would be identified more with its subject than with any one or two institutions. I don't see anything like this happening soon, but I have heard expressions of foundation support for the concept. Having each owner of research collections manage actual resources is more simple, but it may not be the best model for dealing with those in digital format.

Scholars want easy access to vast amounts of research material. Once this was merely wishful thinking. It now may be still naïve, but it is at least possible to consider. I am unaware of anyone working toward such an idea as I suggest, and when it is looked at more closely it may be filled with impossible pitfalls and barriers to its possible success. But the idea is worth exploring. If once we were capable of thinking scholars would sit at their personal computer and write authoritative studies on serious subjects of literature and history and other disciplines, where did we think they were going to get their digital materials? We have it. If all of us put it on servers on our thousands of sites, how long is it going to take these scholars to find what they need? And what standards will be used in digitizing collections? How many researchers will dig deeply to find the kind of material that changes our way of thinking about a subject? Will scholarship suffer even with the proliferation of digital materials on the World Wide Web? It might if we don't think of ways to streamline the process. It is time for us to think about managing this material much as we have thought for a very long time about managing real objects. And the problem is larger when we realize that there are no physical boundaries any more. The problems that are involved in creating shared databases of source materials loom large, to be sure, but if there is any agreement that possible benefits might outweigh them and that the problems of not doing it are no less, then exploring this option seems worthwhile.

The editors of the 50 or so documentary editions of papers now under way in the United States faced some of the same problems recently. Each is producing a collection of papers in book form, almost every one from a different press with an assumed different market (do scholars of the early national period make use of the papers of figures from the late 19th century or the 20th? Not usually, but some scholars would if it were electronic). In an effort to improve access to this information, a pilot project was established. The task of this project, which received funding from the National Historical Publications and Records Commission, the NEH, and a couple of national foundations, has been to find a way to create a master database that would contain all of the electronic files of the various projects' papers. Since the editorial work of verifying text and attaching editorial apparatus is continuing, this project also has as part of its mission designing methods whereby scholarly editors from anywhere on the Internet can do their work electronically, without having to work at a specific place with a specific group of people following a specific daily work schedule. Not only would such a design offer cost savings, it would also open up the possibilities of using the expertise of anyone who might be willing to offer it or become engaged in the work for fee, regardless of their location. Once these collections are on a server, scholars can search any or all of them at once, and the possibilities for new scholarship and new kinds of research are greatly enhanced by the easy access and the virtual singularity of the database.

Resources for this are needed. They are being found individually at sites around the country and abroad, but there seems to be little collaboration and no agreement on uniform standards for research collections. With all we have learned from the advances of scholarship over the past half century, surely there are valuable lessons that might guide us as we engage, almost too rapidly, in this new digital technology and the great promise it offers of bringing our resources to anyone with a connection. The benefits to the advancement of scholarship are almost endless, and with such potential, who is foolish enough to try to stem the tide? We must steer rather than simply cry out from the crow's nest what we see ahead. But the complexity of our future is brought home to us when we realize that at the same time we are steering, someone in the crow's nest had better see any icebergs ahead.

NOTES

1. Douglas Greenberg, "Get Out of the Way If You Can't Lend a Hand: The Changing Nature of Scholarship and the Significance of Special Collections," *Journal of Library Administration,* XIX (1993), 93-95.

2. Thomas Jefferson to Ebenezer Hazard, Feb. 18, 1791, in Boyd et al., The Papers of Thomas Jefferson, XIX, pp. 287.

The Emerging Digital Library:
A New Collaborative Opportunity
on the Academic Campus

Dilawar Grewal
Fred Heath

Historically, research libraries have performed expertly the role of intermediary, linking user communities of scholars and students to the record of scientific research and cultural achievement of humankind. For the past several hundred years, libraries have provided access to information through the acquisition of resources in book or journal form. More recently, only a few years ago, electronic genres were added to the library's role of providing information. While the electronic genres were novel at first, it should be recalled that only a few centuries ago, when first contemplated, the suggestions of printed books displacing the great manuscript libraries of Europe bordered upon the heretical. The coexistence of the book with the manuscript was short lived. Within sixty five years of its opening, the venerable manuscript library of Duke Humfrey was closed by Oxford University and its manuscripts sold. Until the opening of the great Bodleian Library almost half a century later, Oxford's colleges supported the needs of scholarship through the new medium of the printed book, providing scholars with cheaply avail-

Dilawar Grewal is Director, Academy for Advanced Telecommunications and Learning Technologies, Texas A & M University.
Fred Heath is Dean and Director of University Libraries, Texas A & M University.

[Haworth co-indexing entry note]: "The Emerging Digital Library: A New Collaborative Opportunity on the Academic Campus." Grewal, Dilawar, and Fred Heath. Co-published simultaneously in *Journal of Library Administration* (The Haworth Information Press, an imprint of The Haworth Press, Inc.) Vol. 35, No. 3, 2001, pp. 93-105; and: *Impact of Digital Technology on Library Collections and Resource Sharing* (ed: Sul H. Lee) The Haworth Information Press, an imprint of The Haworth Press, Inc., 2001, pp. 93-105. Single or multiple copies of this article are available for a fee from The Haworth Document Delivery Service [1-800-HAWORTH, 9:00 a.m. - 5:00 p.m. (EST). E-mail address: getinfo@haworthpressinc.com].

able information without the expense of contributing to a central library.[1]

And here today, in Oklahoma City, the impact of the digital age upon scholarship is accepted as commonplace. Our colleague from the University of Texas, home of one of the world's great library systems, talked of the "ecosystem" of change; Philip Blackwell spoke of the impact of the digital revolution upon the publishing industry he knows so well, and Karen Hunter of Elsevier openly entertained the concept of the "electronic only" universe that no longer seems as unfathomable or so far away. The question is not whether electronic genres are an important part of scholarship, but rather the extent to which they will transform historical patterns of scholarly communication.

Many of you have seen the following parable most recently offered up by William Wulf, President of the National Academy of Engineering, and AT&T Professor of Computer Science at the University of Virginia. For those of you who have not, it is worth offering here again.

> It's New Year's Day, 1895. My name is Hans. For seven generations my family has made the finest buttons in the region, using the good local horn.
>
> Today I learned that the railroad is coming to our village. My friend Olaf says that cheap factory buttons will come on the trains, but they will never compete with my craftsmanship.
>
> I think he is right, and wrong. They will come, but they *will* compete with my buttons. I must make some choices. I can become a distributor for the new buttons, or I can invest in the machinery to make buttons and export them. Or, closest to my heart, I can refine my craft and sell exceptional buttons to the wealthy.
>
> My family's business is dead. I cannot stop the train. I must change.[2]

If there is a message in this parable of value here today, it is that change brings a range of options. In the digital environment, libraries can abdicate the role of carrying information across time to others more skilled in the processes of data management. Libraries can take up that role themselves, and perform in the digital environment the equivalent role they have performed so well in the print milieu. Or they then take the tools of the digital revolution, and with their particular understanding of the role of libraries in scholarly inquiry, advance the paradigm to newer, more powerful levels. This is a time of opportunity for research libraries and scholarship. Through the digital library, possibilities of new partnerships with scientists and scholars arise that move librarians and librarians from intermediaries to active participants. The information revolution and the digital library are the keys to an exciting era in research librarianship.

THE DIGITAL LIBRARY DEFINED

The Digital Library Federation (DLF) considers digital libraries to be:

> . . . organizations that provide the resources, including the specialized staff, to select, structure, offer intellectual access to, interpret, distribute, preserve the integrity of, and ensure the persistence over time of collections of digital works so that they readily and economically are available for use by a defined community or set of communities.[3]

Certainly this is a workable, functional definition, something all can understand. It is also remarkable for another reason. Look closely and you see that save the insertion of "digital works" it is precisely what research libraries have been doing for over five hundred years. Put another way, in this time of rapid change, evolving standards, and ephemeral software and hardware platforms, no other agency is better prepared than the research library to extend the leadership and provide the vision necessary to carry scholarship forward through time.

The Economics of Collaboration

Today, scholarly communication is still trying to figure out how to come to terms with the digital environment. How does a scholar attain the skills necessary to digitize five thousand year old amphora shards excavated from a wreck on the floor of the Aegean? What about the scans of thousands of fossilized leaves, where evidence of diminishing damage by leaf boring insects across the boundary of the iridium extinction lends credence to the disappearance of the dinosaurs? How will that data, stored by an enterprising young professor on first generation Iomega™ zip drives and left in the credenza of her former office upon her departure for another post, be moved across time? Who attaches the metadata to the digitized specimens in the university herbarium and ensures that the resource can be searched and shared by other herbaria around the world?

The Texas A & M University digital library, founded upon the premise of economies of scale, collaboration, and common purpose, proposes to answer those questions. The expertise emerging in the Digitizing Facility of TAMUDL offers support in the areas of graphics, web-content development, and systems administration and networking. The technical tasks of image acquisition, storage and retrieval are made transparent to the principal investigator or other end user. Individual client compartments are freed from the need to develop personnel expertise or to acquire the high-end equipment required for the imaging activity. From our perspective, centralized imaging and storage resources offer greater cost and planning efficiencies.

The Texas A & M University Digital Library

At Texas A & M University, it is our goal to build a community-wide enterprise in concert with our scholars, researchers and principal investigators as well as with their international network of colleagues. In the recent white paper, Chancellor Billy Frye of Emory University articulated the lofty goal of according scholars access, in the digital environment, to scholarly resources on a magnitude equivalent to the printed resources of the great research libraries of the world:

> Our dream is that all scholarly and research publications (including university, Governmental, research, and museum sites) be universally available on the Internet in perpetuity.[4]

Our vision at Texas A & M University at once embraces that vision and extends it. To some measure, our goal may be born of our own limitations as a library. Texas A & M University Libraries have come lately to embrace the research mission. While there are strengths in our collections, and benefits to be derived from making them available digitally to scholarship, they are not in the aggregate the centerpieces of research on our campus. Rather, those strengths lie in the research activities of faculty: ocean-drilling data, seismic information, meteorology, plant genome data, entomological specimens, pathology research, nautical archeology artifacts and the like. So, rather than scaling a digital enterprise to meet the needs of the libraries, we turned our efforts to a collaborative design with the colleges and the research strengths they represent.

The strategy behind the Texas A & M University Digital Library (TAMUDL) is to build an enterprise level resource for the entire university community. The needs of researchers in the digital environment vary, of course, across disciplines but they also share some things in common, specifically:

- Large-scale storage
- Powerful, brute-force computing
- State-of-the-art imaging equipment
- Sophisticated search and retrieval software

The primary thrust of the Texas A & M University strategy was to design a digital library sufficiently flexible and customizable as to ensure its relevance across a wide range of individual applications. The generic TAMUDL software structure, for example, will address the data handling, interface, and workflow requirements of such diverse applications as Records Management or Electronic Reserves, providing custom applications with necessary features.

THE TEXAS A & M UNIVERSITY
DIGITAL LIBRARY UNFOLDS

Policy Issues

The responsibility of TAMUDL is to ensure that all information acquired and stored in its facilities can be shared across the World Wide Web with other collaborators with full protection of intellectual property rights. Further, that data will be ported across time, and across changing formats and platforms, without regard to the changing priorities and programs of the university itself. Bringing into perspective some of the same values and missions of the print-based research library, TAMUDL has confronted a number of policy issues in its early life:

- What level of autonomy over the data and its structure, its dissemination and layout could be permitted the originator or creator of the data?
- How will users be allowed to customize the look, feel and functionality of their virtual libraries under the main digital library?
- How is it possible to identify common and unique features in the appearance and functionality of various digital library applications in order to build the most efficient infrastructure while still providing for customization needs?

- What are the policy issues relating to the indexing of resident material, and of maintaining diversity and integrity across the entire digital library, which can be composed of many digital libraries?
- How will it be possible to balance user flexibility in design of individual interfaces where deviation from hard coded hooks may be required?
- What will be the policies that govern transition from near on-line storage resources to on-line cache?
- How will TAMUDL govern copyright and other intellectual property issues?

Data Management

TAMUDL is based upon a centralized system management. At the same time, *content management* resides with the originator of the data, who is responsible for its appearance and intellectual value.

- All data requiring indexing will be resident on the digital library servers.
- All aspects of the digital library will be Web accessible. Aspects include data acquisition or ingest, administration, and search and retrieval.
- While hyperlinks to external sites will be supported, indexing on those sites will not be undertaken. (This policy rule was established for the benefit of the search engine and to ensure integrity of data resident on the digital library servers.)
- The digital library search engine will allow for simultaneous searches over metadata, full-text, and by using the images themselves as queries.
- When employing image queries, a user will be able to dictate the granularity of the search and assign weights to search parameters such as local color, global color, texture, and structure.
- Encoded video will be made searchable by the full-text search engine, indexing video using voice-to-text engines. Text from embedded captions and teletext would also be part of the searchable index.
- Capability to search video using image queries exists but will not be deployed initially.
- While the entire digital library will be searchable, security provisions will allow originators of data to control all or parts of their virtual libraries, restricting accessibility for browsing and/or searching by others.
- Workflow or asset management systems will be available for clients to engage.

Solution Architecture

TAMUDL is a complex blend of hardware platforms and software solutions. The following paragraphs are intended to give a feel for the various components integral to its operation.

Server Side. On the server side, TAMUDL is supported by a Silicon Graphics (SGI) Origin 2000 enterprise level server with 10 processors, two gigabytes of RAM, and Fiber channel RAID with one terabyte of online disk storage and cache. It is supported by an EMASS robotic tape array with 16 AIT drives with 60 terabytes of tape storage capacity. In addition, there exist Windows and Apple platform-based servers that host project-specific services software. Such services can be engaged as required by individual virtual libraries. Examples include: watermarking software, voice-to-text conversion (to make video searchable by full-text engines), electronic signatures, etc.

Server side software has two major branches dealing with digital assets: Search/Browse components and Asset Importing components. Figure 1 illustrates the Search/Browse component architecture.

FIGURE 1. Search/Browse Component Architecture

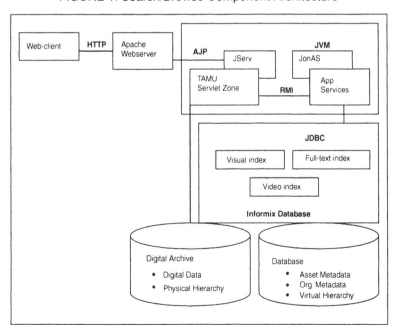

Constituents of the Search/Browse component architecture and their functions are described below:

- APP–This is a Digital Asset Management application that is engaged for importing digital assets, organizing collections, and browsing and searching the collections. It uses Informix database tables for storage and uses the full-text, visual indexing, and video indexing blades for creating image signatures, video logging, voice-to-text conversion, and full-text indexing. This application is the basis for the entire solution architecture.
- JonAS–The APP services are implemented using Enterprise Java Beans. JonAS is an application server that provides the engine to execute the services on behalf of the client. The beans issue SQL calls to the database or the database blades through the Java Database Connectivity (JDBC) protocol.
- Apache and Jserv–The Apache Web server receives and responds to user requests across the Web. The client submits a Uniform Resource Locator (URL) to Apache. If the URL corresponds to a physical pathname, Apache returns the file's contents over the Internet to the client. If the URL corresponds to a service, Apache passes the request to the servlet engine Jserv, through the Apache Jserv Protocol. Jserv then finds the corresponding servlet, executes the servlet, and returns the results of the servlet to the client across the Internet. Both requests from the client and responses from the server are encoded using HTTP.
- TAMU Servlet Zone–The TAMU Servlet Zone contains the servlets that provide the client interface to the APP. These include the servlets for searching, browsing, session management, and security services.
- Java–Almost all Java servlets, applications, and services execute from a common Java Virtual Machine (JVM). Exceptions to this are the database Java Services, which execute from a database JVM.
- The Service Broker–The Service Broker is an application server that imports assets into the system. It uses a table driven parser to determine file types, and then to execute the services that are needed to import files representing the data portion for an asset.
- Services Pool–The services Pool contains the various services that the Service Broker calls upon while importing digital media into the TAMUDL. The pool contains services for inserting asset

metadata, creating thumbnails or lower resolution images, and obtaining visual image signatures for images.
- Services Servers–External Apple and Windows servers run applications to process images for custom applications. Examples of such applications would include putting watermarking information or electronic signatures, routing images through converters, etc.

For each new virtual library that is created in TAMUDL, a directory structure is created for the import and approval of assets. Along with creating the directory structure, the rules governing the access of assets from these directories, any users or user groups and their security levels, and any workflow related protocols are established. Configuration files for the Services in the Services Pool and the APP services are created to define custom services and workflow for individual libraries. A conduit for external manipulation of data is provided via the service broker to applications running on external Windows or Apple servers as seen in Figure 2.

FIGURE 2. Digital Asset Importation Engine Architecture

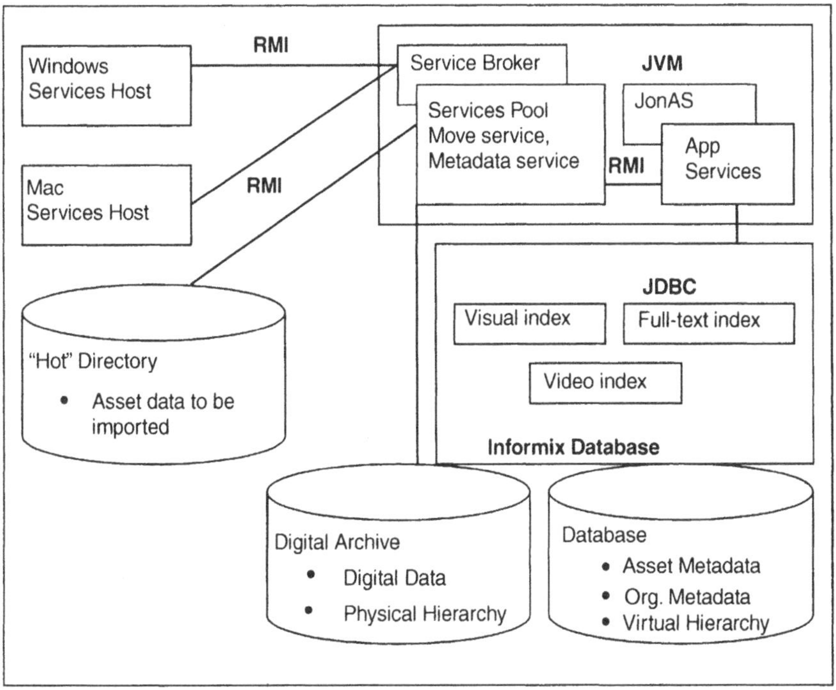

Also a "hot directory" is created which is the final point of submission for the assets to be ingested into the virtual library. Once the material is submitted to the "hot directory" the Service Broker takes over and performs the appropriate actions on the data. These actions and services are defined in the configuration files established for that individual virtual library. In operation, the Service Broker engages a "listener" to scan the "hot directory" for digital materials to import. Using a table driven parser, the Service Broker attempts to categorize each file it encounters. The table uses both the file extensions, together with the initial bytes read from the file to make the determination. Each file type known to the system is associated with an asset route that is a list of services to be applied to the asset or to one of its derivatives. For example, one service can create a thumbnail image for the asset, while another could read the asset's metadata from a file and write it into the tables. Subsequently, all material is processed for metadata, full-text and VIR indexing. While the asset and organizational metadata is stored in database tables, along with a virtual hierarchy, the actual digital assets are stored outside of the database. This helps with efficiency issues, and also with limiting the amount of time the database Concurrent License is engaged.

On the Search/Browse/Retrieval end of the operation, customization for individual virtual libraries takes place in the form of custom access, based upon users and access rights for them as well as the entire world, and also customization of the results pages. For the final customized look and feel of a virtual library the use of "disguises" is invoked. User defined graphical interfaces are used to provide the look and functionality for that particular virtual library, based upon the table structure in the database. Even though each library relates back to the same set of tables in the database being used by TAMUDL, individual disguises allow for the customization of the labels and the number of visible fields, their layout, etc. For example, a field–NAME–could be listed as Author Name for one virtual library and as Creator for another virtual library, thus providing a custom user interface for each application.

Client Side. Java enabled Web browsers are used as the client-side interface for search, browse and even administrative tasks. No application download is required. In case of specific applications, as defined by a workflow needing to be run on the client side, Java applets are engaged. For generic browsing and searching, users do not need a login. Everything that has the access rights set for worldview is available. However, for restricted parts of virtual libraries, login with pre-established userids is required for both browsing and searching. Also, once a user is logged in, the security, access and workflow protocols govern the functionality available to that user within that virtual library.

For the virtual libraries available to general users, a user can either choose all available or choose a collection of virtual libraries or parts thereof, for searching. There are two ways a user can conduct searches on TAMUDL. A textual search can be conducted on either the metadata, full-text or both. Another method available is to use either an image from the existing libraries or imported from a local source as an image query source. All returned results illustrate their source and any parent-child relationships with other assets. Also, depending upon the security rights, results returned can be emailed, ftp'd or routed, if a workflow has been established.

To enable efficient retrieval of assets over the Internet, smart and read-ahead caching is employed to populate the terabyte cache. This also includes caching dormant materials once accessed by a search engine.

SALIENT FEATURES OF TAMUDL

As the above architectural design amply demonstrates, the purpose of TAMUDL is to bring high-end solutions to even the smallest projects within reach of principal investigators, researchers and educators. The investment in TAMUDL is intended to make transparent to end-users most of the technical issues surrounding the development, organization, and maintenance of large data sets. Ubiquity of access is assured by Web-accessibility of most functions, including the acquisition and ingest of data, administration, routing of documents and search and retrieval. Workflow Control can include engaging a Media Asset Management System (MAMS) for routing, time stamping, and annotations. Intellectual content can be protected by watermarking, traceable electronic signatures and other means.

Documents can be accepted as scanned-in images, text documents, and also as electronic documents with both text and embedded images. In case of electronic documents with both text and images, built in parsers separate the two types of data and index them individually. Textual data can be searched both by metadata added by the researchers or by optical character recognition of text in the images. Query by image content can also be supported. A schoolchild searching the public database of butterflies in an entomological collection mounted on the server can select an image of a yellow butterfly and direct TAMUDL to select other images from the large file to display other, similar images. In this way, it would be possible to match the specimen in the schoolroom to the matching image in the database. Searches on local color, global color, texture and structure have application in a range of sophisticated scientific applications.

Central to the future of TAMUDL is the care and maintenance of the facility itself. Just as research libraries have carried out their responsibility for carrying information across time through responsible stewardship involving the maintenance of facilities to correctly house print resources, on-going budgets to acquire them, and the special skills required to conserve them, so too must digital libraries be likewise equipped. TAMUDL has been assembled through a wide range of external grants. Major funding for equipment has been obtained from the Texas Telecommunication Infrastructure Board and from Ford Motor Company. Software development was achieved in partnership with Silicon Graphics, Inc. (SGI). Altogether, the sum of start-up funds for the development of the facility amount to nearly a million dollars. The contributed costs and development expertise of partners such as Silicon Graphics add a like amount to that total. The business plan for TAMUDL is based upon sufficient resources to replace its hardware and software on an on-going basis and to provide for sufficient staff to ensure its effective operation. Support from the colleges at Texas A & M University provided the start-up operating capital; on-going support is envisaged from technology fees that will enhance student access to distance learning, electronic reserves and classroom instruction.

Benefits

The design team responsible for the Texas A & M University Digital Library approached it as a challenge that had to be met out of the box. This included both an evaluation of paradigms, as well as portability and applicability of the final product for multiple and diverse uses. Some benefits of implementing such a design include facilitation of research collaboration across distances. Most researchers occupy specialties whose closest collaborators may be at other institutions or laboratories. The web-based features of TAMUDL, with its layers of security and intellectual property protection, optimize the possibilities for data-sharing and information exchange. It provides an affordable infrastructure for applications such as learning-on-demand, distance education, and collaborative research in a distributive environment.

The high-end resources facilitate the creation and management of the content-specific areas of expertise that characterize the nature of research on a university campus, bringing powerful tools to the use of researchers, teachers and students. Drawing upon the skills and resources of the center, experts are able to focus on building their digital collections rather than concerning themselves with the operation and maintenance of the requisite hardware and software. Most important of all, it provides these powerful tools to its clientele without requiring them to conform to a rigid set of profiles. TAMUDL also extends some degree of perpetuity to the maintenance of digital assets. The fundamental commitment of TAMUDL is that resources managed by the facility will be carried across time without regard to changing formats or platforms, or even shifts in university priorities. While that commitment has yet to stand the test of time so evident in research libraries, it is apparent that campus-based resources such as TAMUDL are more likely to withstand that test than commercial or other out-sourcing options for the permanent archiving of digital data.

SUMMARY

Providing and maintaining digital content online can be a complex and expensive proposition. However, choosing the right delivery vehicle and designing it as a flexible and versatile tool can be useful in securing maximum leverage across a multitude of applications and projects. A well-designed Digital Library can be such a tool, providing the appropriate vehicle for delivery of online information under diverse requirements. Hopefully the various issues identified in this paper will resonate at various levels with many users and designers of digital asset management systems and provide valuable insight into designing online information delivery vehicles out of the box.

REFERENCES

1. Rogers, D. *The Bodleian Library and Its Treasures: 1320-1700.* Nuffield, Henley-on-Thames: Aidan Ellis, p. 9.

2. This parable often used by the author can be found in Wulf, W. (1995). Warning: Information technology will transform the university. *Issues in Science and Technology, the Quarterly Publication of the National Academy of Science.* 11 (4), p. 46.

3. Digital Library Federation. A working definition. Available at <http:www: clir.org/diglib/dldefinition.htm>.

4. Battin, P., Campbell, J., Frye, B., Hawkins, B., Kaufman, P., Lynch, C., & West, R. *Assuring Library Resources for the new millennium.* Emory University, January 10, 2001, p. 1.

Copyright and Intellectual Property Legislation and Related Activities: New Challenges for Libraries

Prudence Adler

Yogi Berra once noted that "the future ain't what it used to be." Qualifying his statement he said, "I just meant that times are different. Not necessarily better or worse. Just different."[1] This may characterize where we find ourselves in trying to apply library values such as privacy and the balancing of interests in intellectual property and copyright law with fast-paced technological change and the new reality of e-commerce and the information age. Our collections or content have been transformed into "information" and "knowledge." This is the "new" commodity that has all sectors scrambling to explore and develop new marketplace models. In addition to the different perspectives, there are new voices with other views in addition to technologies that place new limitations on how content may be used, shared, and sold.

A review of key federal and state legislation, court cases, and emerging technologies might provide a different context to these discussions, and it might also shed some light on this unsettled arena in which we find ourselves. By stepping back from the immediacy of each court case or legislative proposal, we might see how these shifting information policies will affect research libraries in the years ahead. And it may assist in sorting through how to match our values and policy interests

---

Prudence Adler is Associate Executive Director of Federal Relations & Information Policy, ARL, Washington, DC.

[Haworth co-indexing entry note]: "Copyright and Intellectual Property Legislation and Related Activities: New Challenges for Libraries." Adler, Prudence. Co-published simultaneously in *Journal of Library Administration* (The Haworth Information Press, an imprint of The Haworth Press, Inc.) Vol. 35, No. 3, 2001, pp. 107-118; and: *Impact of Digital Technology on Library Collections and Resource Sharing* (ed: Sul H. Lee) The Haworth Information Press, an imprint of The Haworth Press, Inc., 2001, pp. 107-118.

against the allure and appeal of the Internet and the Web with the reality of the offerings.

Intellectual property and copyright policies have been and will continue to be central to our communities. This is not a surprise. Historically, the research, education, and library communities have looked to copyright law as the policy framework for balancing the competing interests of creators, publishers, and users of copyrighted works. But this balance is being challenged in a number of arenas–in Congress, in the courts, through contractual arrangements, and more recently, through the introduction of technological protection measures.

The advent of the Internet, the World Wide Web, and digital technologies as platforms for the distribution of information products dramatically altered how owners and creators of information permit access to these resources. It has also spawned opportunities as well pitfalls for users and owners alike. The drive to be responsive to the E-commerce call results in many companies being focused on the secure distribution of their content. This has lead to a shift in emphasis–towards marketplace or economic concerns versus the balancing of societal and economic interests in promoting access to information resources.

There is a direct correlation between the concerns regarding the ease of copying and redistributing digital content and the growing reliance upon licenses, technological protection measures, and a shift in how Congress approaches protection of intellectual property. Yes, the reality is that copying and redistribution of electronic resources is significantly improved with digital technologies but the massive harm and rampant piracy claimed by proponents of heightened intellectual property protection has been a clever means to achieve what was previously not attainable–new legislation and proposals that eviscerate the balance of the Copyright Act.

The press to change the copyright and intellectual property framework is occurring in a number of venues. In the past few years, Congress has enacted the No Electronic Theft "Net" Act of 1997, the Digital Millennium Copyright Act (DMCA) that includes the Sony Bono Term Extension Act, online service provider liability provisions, and has been actively considering database legislation. And more is on the agenda for the 107th Congress. The move away from copyright as the primary legal and policy framework to licensing is also reflected in the recent push to adopt UCITA, the Uniform Computer Information Transactions Act. Finally, there are a growing number of challenges in the courts that are defining and refining rights and privileges in the digital environment.

CONGRESSIONAL ACTIVITIES

Following years of detailed and extremely contentious debates, Congress passed the Digital Millennium Copyright Act in October 1998. Key issues addressed in this copyright update include: access to and fair use of copyrighted works issued in encrypted form, the liability of online service providers for infringing behavior by a user of the service, the proper uses of copyrighted works in distance education programs, the extension of the term of protection of copyrighted works, and the use of digital technology to preserve library and archival materials.

Congress delayed implementation of several of these provisions (fair use of encrypted works or section 1201 and issues relating to the first sale doctrine) pending further study and consideration, and not surprisingly, these were some of the most contentious issues. The Librarian of Congress, the Copyright Office, and the Assistant Secretary of the Department of Commerce were tasked with undertaking these reviews. The comments made by different sectors during the rulemaking provide striking insights into the marketplace models of different industries. For example, comments made by Streambox TV were very similar to those of the library and education communities. Streambox technologies allows consumers to record live and on demand streaming content for later use. Bob Hildeman of Streambox stated, "there is no doubt that the protection of fair use rights in the digital realm would be a benefit to content owners, consumers and companies such as Streambox."[2] The shared view, of course, is that fair use is needed to support innovation and the evolution of the Internet.

Other voices include those of traditional content providers such as the Recording Industry Association of America (RIAA). Cary Sherman of RIAA commented that "with digital rights management, you would be able to sell a single listen or a week of listens or a month of listens or a rental thing, where after a certain point, you can buy it for a small additional price. And digital rights management systems are very flexible ways of implementing those business models, and that's why they'll be a key element in electronic delivery systems in the future." Another example of the radically different approach is the position of Microsoft that sees fair use as "a 'cop-out . . . a giant escape clause' from copyright laws that allow owners to control the copying of their property."[3] Finally, Peter Chernin, President of News Corp. recently called for new legislation that "guarantees publishers' control of not only the integrity of an original work, but of the extent and duration of users' access to that work, the availability of data about the work and restrictions on forwarding the work to others." This is a very different view of access to resources than ours, yet it is the new market reality that we need to understand in order to apply our values and achieve our missions.[4]

Provisions in the DMCA relating to technological measures refers to those technologies that can determine who can use a resource and when and how that resource can be used. For example, can a user copy, extract, print, loan, and/or archive the resource? Under the Copyright Act, certain privileges and exemptions permit these activities. With a technological protection measure, the user no longer has those choices; indeed, the owner or publisher of the work determines which, if any, uses are permitted. Thus the dilemma. Under the doctrine of fair use and other library and education exemptions, certain unauthorized use is permitted. The notion is that permission is not required for each and every use. Yet under DMCA, unauthorized circumventing of a technological protection measure is illegal, thus the view of some that there is no fair use in a world that employs technological protection measures.

Unfortunately, the Librarian of Congress, with advice from the Copyright Office, issued a deeply disappointing ruling that many view as restricting access to information by the public. Why such a harsh view? Whereas members of the education, research, and library communities were strong advocates for a broad exemption to permit fair use to be exercised in the networked environment, the Librarian and the Copyright Office did not propose such an exemption. In contrast, the Assistant Secretary of Commerce called for exemptions "grounded in the principle of fair use" that would allow the public to fully realize their access to lawfully acquired information. As a result, if there is a technological protection measure or TPM associated with a work, that TPM can prohibit a user from exercising fair use, first sale, and more.

A related study by the Copyright Office and Department of Commerce study, again mandated by Congress in the DMCA, is examining the first sale doctrine and related issues in the digital environment. In testimony before the Copyright Office, the library community noted that with the implementation of the DMCA, the first sale doctrine is diminished and the ability of libraries to support the legitimate information access needs of their users is undermined. At the same time, the ability of publishers to monitor and control use of works is greatly expanded. Predictably, content providers saw no need for a change in statute. Allan Adler of the Association of American Publishers noted that no change was needed, indeed should not be considered, as any changes to the statute could thwart the success of new marketplace models such as NetLibrary and Questia.

Legislation to provide additional protections to databases first surfaced in the United States in 1996. The legislation resulted from a combination of factors. First, some in the information industry reacted to the EU Directive on the legal protection of databases. The reciprocity card–the notion that databases created in non-EC countries would not be granted legal protection–prompted some segments of the database industry to advocate the need for additional protection. In addition, there was a 1991 Supreme Court ruling, called Feist v. Rural Telephone. For those database publishers who relied on the concept of "sweat of the brow" or looking to investment as a measure of protection, this ruling marked the need to look elsewhere. This ruling continues to overshadow the impact of the EU directive and is at the heart of the U.S. discussions.

Why? Because the Court reaffirmed the United States perspective that copyright and creative expression–be it selection, organization, or original authorship–are the basis for protection in our system. Thus investment was not and could not be a standard that publishers could rely upon. Moreover, under this framework, facts included in a database would always remain in the public domain regardless of the amount invested in the database. And, because this decision is grounded in the Constitution, to "promote the progress of Science and the Useful Arts," any new legislation in this arena has very high constitutional hurdles to contend with.[5]

From the very beginning of discussions in the U.S., the database proposal has been controversial. Indeed, each year, the proposed legislation has been mired in controversy as more and more communities appreciate the consequences of the legislation regarding how they conduct research and/or business. In fact, one participant in the debates noted that the impact of the database legislation on science and research would be similar to the asteroid hitting Earth in the movie Armaggedon. Between 1996 and today, database protection legislation has inched forward and is now, in effect, at a stalemate.

One of the more interesting aspects of this difficult debate is how the various communities have reacted to the legislation. In 1996, members of the scientific and library communities and a few database producers such as Dun & Bradstreet opposed the passage of database legislation. By 1998, this debate changed as many in higher education appreciated the risks associated with a sweeping change to database protection. As users and creators of information, these communities require balanced policies regarding creation, use, and dissemination of information. Since that time, we've witnessed a surge in the number of commercial and non-commercial sectors actively participating in this debate. And I should note, some of our partners are very strange bedfellows indeed.

Virtually all of higher education, science, and libraries support a limited, targeted, balanced approach to database protection. We are joined by many telecommunications partners such as AT&T, Verizon, and MCI WorldCom. Some of the most vocal critics of strong protections are the portals such as Yahoo! Inc., AOL Time Warner, Excite@Home, Amazon.com, Inc., Inktomi, and more. Financial services companies such as Bloomberg Financial Markets, Charles Schwab & Co., Inc., Reuters America Inc., and others believe that the combination of copyright, contract law, and technological protections provide sufficient protection, thus a narrowly focused bill, if any, is all that is required. Rarely will you see these competitors working together, let alone united on a piece of legislation.

What concerns do these companies share with higher education, libraries, and the research and scientific communities? As diverse as our coalition is with over 140 groups and companies, we share deep-seated concerns regarding the different approaches to database legislation. Although libraries, AT&T, the U.S. Chamber of Commerce, the Consumers Union, the Eagle Forum, and Yahoo have in some cases different value sets and perspectives that they bring to this debate, all view facts as the building blocks of knowledge or of e-commerce. All license or purchase data and are not "free riders." For example, every year, the non-profit library community licenses and/or acquires, well over $2 billion of information resources. Similarly, Yahoo licenses a myriad of resources in order to attract and retain customers.

Another shared perspective is the valid concern about creating monopoly control over information. From the perspective of the library community, the database protection debate is directly related to issues with the current system of scholarly communication.

- There is a growing gap between the price of information and the ability to pay.
- There is an explosion in knowledge, both in formats and volume.
- There is a consolidation in the publishing industry.
- We are faced with different and diverging cultures–the circle of gifts vs. the market economy. We cannot support proposals that would provide greater control over information, how it is used, and what it costs.

For the telecommunications providers, a uniting factor has been sim-ply not knowing what business models they will be pursuing in a few years. Thus they do not want to agree to a legal regime which may dis-advantage them or spark anti-competitive activities. In addition, they are deeply concerned about liability issues. How, for example, would one determine liability for serving as a conduit for "facts"? How would a provider know who was the owner of a fact? This holds true for librar-ies and higher education institutions as well as Internet Service Pro-viders.

THE SHIFT TO LICENSING

As noted by Mary Case in the ARL Licensing Workshops, economic, technical, legal, and market factors resulted in an unsettled environment for electronic publishing. This uncertainty gave rise to the increasing re-liance by publishers upon licenses in lieu of copyright law. The new framework includes new players such as aggregators and consortia, and new publishers and vendors. The legal regimes include contract law, trade secret law, state law, and copyright law. The most recent entrant is UCITA.

UCITA is a proposed state law that seeks to create a unified approach to the licensing of software and information. Two states–Maryland and Virginia–have passed UCITA, and it is under active consideration in many other states including Illinois, Texas, and Arizona. UCITA's broad scope and focus requires that the research, education, and library communities understand what the adoption of UCITA will mean for the mission, operation, and core values of the higher education and library communities. All facets of the research, education, and library enter-prise rely upon software and information to create and disseminate knowledge. Indeed, members of these communities are both users and creators of these products and services and are among the largest con-sumers of information and software. Historically, the research, educa-tion, and library communities have looked to copyright law as the policy framework for balancing competing interests of the creators, publishers, and users of copyrighted works. UCITA will dramatically change this framework.

As noted in a letter to members of the Maryland General Assembly from leading intellectual property faculty:

until recently, federal copyright law and contract law have co-existed in relative harmony. Effectively, only copyright law governed works generally distributed to the public, while works with limited distribution could receive both copyright and contract protection. More recently however, software companies began distributing their products to the general public subject to shrinkwrap licenses.[6]

As the use of shrinkwrap licenses by publishers grew, a subtle but important legal shift occurred. Courts previously skeptical of shrinkwrap or click-on licenses became more supportive. UCITA codifies this growing, but not universal, acceptance by legalizing the use of click-on, non-negotiated licenses. The potential result will be the displacement of the uniform system under federal copyright law (that seeks appropriate balances between creators, users, and publishers) with a contract-based system that will operate under the flawed assumption that there is a level playing field between licensors and licensees. This will not be the case for shrinkwrap licenses where the licensor unilaterally sets the terms.

Since the inception of the digital environment, copyright has applied to digital works and the Internet. Proponents of UCITA claim that there is a need to provide a new legal framework to address digital issues, completely ignoring the DMCA and existing copyright case law. UCITA thus represents an end-run around the DMCA and the Copyright Act as interpreted by the federal courts. This proposal is a means to implement on a state level what UCITA proponents have not achieved on the federal level. UCITA creates a very different approach to intellectual property protection with no exemptions and fair use defenses for the research, education, and library communities.[7]

SELECTED COURT CASES

Increasingly, Courts have become the venue for resolution of many copyright and intellectual property issues. And with the enactment of DMCA, we have seen a rise in the number of cases before the Courts with the prediction of many, many more to come. Three cases are of particular interest to these discussions: *Tasini v. The New York Times, Universal City Studios v. Eric Corley, A/K/A Emmanuel Goldstein and 2600 Enterprises, Inc.,* and *Eldred v. Reno.* ARL and ALA have filed amicus briefs in two of these cases, sometimes with partners to provide the perspective of the library and non-profit communities.

What is the *Tasini* case? In September 1999, the U.S. Court of Appeals for the Second Circuit, in a unanimous ruling, overturned a lower court decision in the case of *Tasini v. The New York Times*. The lower court had held that the defendant-publishers had the right to include the work of freelance writers in the full-text databases the publishers licensed to vendors, even without a contract with the freelance writers that specifically granted the rights for further publication. In reversing the lower court ruling, the appeals court ruled that the reuse of a freelance author's work on CD-ROMs and in electronic databases without the author's permission constitutes copyright infringement.

The New York Times and the other publishers who had been sued (including *Newsday* and *Time*) then asked the appellate court to grant a full-court ("en banc") review of the panel decision, but the Second Circuit rejected that request in April 2000. The case is now before the U.S. Supreme Court.

What are the implications of the case for libraries? Although many publications such as the *The New York Times* now require permission for electronic republication of works by freelance authors, this was not standard industry practice until recently. Thus the impact of the ruling primarily will be on older works–over the last 20 years–currently residing in databases such as Lexis-Nexis and the like. Commercial electronic database publishers claim that the decision of the Appeals Court forces them to delete articles by freelance writers in their databases. They also claim that it would not be feasible to remunerate the authors due to the large number of works involved as well as the expense of locating these contributors.

For many freelance writers, the appellate ruling that found in favor of the authors (led by Jonathan Tasini, President of the National Writers Union) represents a fair decision that helps to rectify past problems. Authors in this case have not asked that their articles be deleted from the commercial electronic databases; instead they seek fair compensation.

In providing a library perspective, ARL and ALA suggested that there are constructive ways for the Court to address the concerns of this case that are fair to both freelance authors, the commercial electronic database producers, and the public. Freelance authors should be compensated for their work, but the public interest in having access to these materials should also be recognized and respected–without having to create a crisis that the publishers suggest is inevitable if the freelance authors are successful in the case. A solution could be a system of payment to freelance writers which would result in a complete and historical record in many formats. Such a solution would further the public interest in access to these works. I should also note that ARL and ALA took the occasion to provide the Court with information concerning preservation and access issues as the *The New York Times*, Lexis, and others view these commercial electronic databases as archival media replacing libraries.[8]

Why the interest in the DVD case? There are significant implications for library and educational institutions concerning linking to Internet sites and the potential liability of these institutions. The defendant, "2600: The Hacker Quarterly," posted on its web site the computer program for decrypting and copying movies on DVDs. As DVDs are protected by technological protection measures, this action, to some, seemed to run afoul of provisions in DMCA. The Court ruled that the defendants could not post the decrypting information as well as link to that information at other sites.

As links are an essential and fundamental element of the Web, a court ruling in this arena has ramifications for both the usefulness of the Web as currently constructed, as well as for its evolution. In his ruling, Judge Kaplan noted concern over the possible effect of his ruling on the Web. To address First Amendment concerns, he established a test to determine if, when linking to a site that contains information that is considered illegal under DMCA, (1) the institution or "linker" knew that there was illegal information on the site, (2) knew that the information should not have been offered, and (3) finally, deliberately linked to the site to make information available.[9]

Finally, the case *Eldred v. Reno* challenged the constitutionality of the "Sony Bono Term Extension Act." The Court determined that extensions are within Congress' authority under the Copyright Clause and that the 20-year extension did not violate the First Amendment. This new extension, characterized by Peter Jaszi as "perpetual protection on an installment plan," will result in fewer works moving into the public domain. This will influence a number of library activities–for example, how these resources are used, which may be digitized (outside the scope of fair use), whether to engage in a costly permissions process, and the like. All of this leads to additional costs to the libraries and less access to information resources by our users.

CONCLUSION

Continuing with the baseball theme, Wes Westrum, a former manager of the Mets said, "Baseball is like church. Many attend but few understand."[10] The same could be said for the details of copyright and intellectual property. But some themes emerge from the overview of copyright and intellectual property issues.

First, there has been a noted shift in the balance between owners, users, and creators of information. The new provisions in DMCA favor the owners of information at the expense of the users of information. The press for enactment of UCITA is another example of this shift as UCITA provides significant new leverage to the licensor, not the licensee. This represents a greater focus on economic interests and less on societal interests, again the allure with promoting, stimulating, and protecting e-commerce. Challenges such as *Tasini v The New York Times, Eldred v. Reno,* and many others represent an attempt to restore balance to the system.

Second, the most controversial proposals–the anti-circumvention provisions, database protection legislation, and UCITA–are outside of copyright or as some refer to them as "paracopyright." The new technological protections measures in DMCA are "add-ons" if you will, and fall outside the scope of the balanced approach taken in the Copyright Act.

Third, there are new voices and partners to engage in these debates. As the database discussions and the Copyright Office rulemaking demonstrate, there are other fellow travelers we should seek out and work with to moderate or defeat some of the more problematic proposals. And we should work with these communities to promote a positive agenda concerning access to information in the networked environment.

Fourth, an important theme that runs through many of these discussions is the need for harmonization–harmonization with the European Union concerning database protection, global harmonization regarding new copyright treaties, and harmonization across the states through UCITA.

Finally, last week I received an e-mail from Paula Kaufman who noted that these "ip wars" went to the heart of what we are trying to accomplish. They do challenge our values and our ability to carry out our missions effectively. For faculty, library users, students, and staff the complexity of managing and accessing information will grow if we continue to move into more restrictive legal environments. The investments made in collection development, cooperative and collaborative endeavors will not be realized unless we establish balanced intellectual property regimes that support research and education as well as the interests of owners of intellectual property.

REFERENCES

1. Berra, Yogi, *The Yogi Book*, Workman Publishing, New York, pages 118-119.

2. Library of Congress, United States Copyright Office, Hearing on Exemption to Prohibition on Circumvention of Copyright Protection Systems for Access Control Technologies, Washington, D.C., May 3, 2000, <http://www.loc.gov/copyright/1201/hearings/index.html#transcripts>.

3. Munro, Neil, "A Window Into Microsoft's Strategy," *National Journal*, 10/21/3000, page 3337.

4. Milliot, Jim, "Copyright Protection Stressed at AAP Meeting," <http://www.publishersweekly.com/articles>.

5. Feist, 499 at 349-50.

The U.S. Supreme Court in Feist states, "It may seem unfair that much of the fruit of the compiler's labor may be used by others without compensation. As Justice Brennan has correctly observed, however, this is not 'some unforeseen by product of a statutory scheme.' It is, rather, 'the essence of copyright,' and a constitutional requirement. The primary objective of copyright is not to reward the labor of authors, but 'to promote the Progress of Science and useful Arts.' To this end, copyright assures the authors the right to their original expression, but encourages others to build freely upon the ideas and information conveyed by a work . . . This result is neither unfair nor unfortunate. It is the means by which copyright advances the progress of science and art."

6. See <http://www.arl.org/info/letters/profs_ucita.html>.

7. For more information on UCITA, please see, Association of Research Libraries, "UCITA: Summary and Implications for Libraries and Higher Education," Washington, D.C., Fall 2000, <http://www.arl.org/info/frn/copy/ucitasum.html>.

8. For more information, please see ARL/ALA amicus brief: <http://www.arl.org/info/frn/copy/tasini.html>.

9. Kaplan, Carol C., "Assessing Linking Liability," *New York Times*, 9.8.2000, <http://www.nytimes.com/2000/09/08/technology/08CYBERLAW.html>.

10. Running Press, *Baseball Wit and Wisdom*, Philadelphia, 1992.

Index

Integrating Total Quality Management in a Library Setting, edited by Susan Jurow, MLS, and Susan B. Barnard, MLS (Vol. 18, No. 1/2, 1993). *"Especially valuable are the librarian experiences that directly relate to real concerns about TQM. Recommended for all professional reading collections." (Library Journal)*

Leadership in Academic Libraries: Proceedings of the W. Porter Kellam Conference, The University of Georgia, May 7, 1991, edited by William Gray Potter (Vol. 17, No. 4, 1993). *"Will be of interest to those concerned with the history of American academic libraries." (Australian Library Review)*

Collection Assessment and Acquisitions Budgets, edited by Sul H. Lee (Vol. 17, No. 2, 1993). *Contains timely information about the assessment of academic library collections and the relationship of collection assessment to acquisition budgets.*

Developing Library Staff for the 21st Century, edited by Maureen Sullivan (Vol. 17, No. 1, 1992). *"I found myself enthralled with this highly readable publication. It is one of those rare compilations that manages to successfully integrate current general management operational thinking in the context of academic library management." (Bimonthly Review of Law Books)*

Vendor Evaluation and Acquisition Budgets, edited by Sul H. Lee (Vol. 16, No. 3, 1992). *"The title doesn't do justice to the true scope of this excellent collection of papers delivered at the sixth annual conference on library acquisitions sponsored by the University of Oklahoma Libraries." (Kent K. Hendrickson, BS, MALS, Dean of Libraries, University of Nebraska-Lincoln) Find insightful discussions on the impact of rising costs on library budgets and management in this groundbreaking book.*

The Management of Library and Information Studies Education, edited by Herman L. Totten, PhD, MLS (Vol. 16, No. 1/2, 1992). *"Offers something of interest to everyone connected with LIS education–the undergraduate contemplating a master's degree, the doctoral student struggling with courses and career choices, the new faculty member aghast at conflicting responsibilities, the experienced but stressed LIS professor, and directors of LIS Schools." (Education Libraries)*

Library Management in the Information Technology Environment: Issues, Policies, and Practice for Administrators, edited by Brice G. Hobrock, PhD, MLS (Vol. 15, No. 3/4, 1992). *"A road map to identify some of the alternative routes to the electronic library." (Stephen Rollins, Associate Dean for Library Services, General Library, University of New Mexico)*

Managing Technical Services in the 90's, edited by Drew Racine (Vol. 15, No. 1/2, 1991). *"Presents an eclectic overview of the challenges currently facing all library technical services efforts. . . . Recommended to library administrators and interested practitioners." (Library Journal)*

Budgets for Acquisitions: Strategies for Serials, Monographs, and Electronic Formats, edited by Sul H. Lee (Vol. 14, No. 3, 1991). *"Much more than a series of handy tips for the careful shopper. This [book] is a most useful one–well-informed, thought-provoking, and authoritative." (Australian Library Review)*

Creative Planning for Library Administration: Leadership for the Future, edited by Kent Hendrickson, MALS (Vol. 14, No. 2, 1991). *"Provides some essential information on the planning process, and the mix of opinions and methodologies, as well as examples relevant to every library manager, resulting in a very readable foray into a topic too long avoided by many of us." (Canadian Library Journal)*

Strategic Planning in Higher Education: Implementing New Roles for the Academic Library, edited by James F. Williams, II, MLS (Vol. 13, No. 3/4, 1991). *"A welcome addition to the sparse literature on strategic planning in university libraries. Academic librarians considering strategic planning for their libraries will learn a great deal from this work." (Canadian Library Journal)*

Personnel Administration in an Automated Environment, edited by Philip E. Leinbach, MLS (Vol. 13, No. 1/2, 1990). *"An interesting and worthwhile volume, recommended to university library administrators and to others interested in thought-provoking discussion of the personnel implications of automation." (Canadian Library Journal)*

Library Development: A Future Imperative, edited by Dwight F. Burlingame, PhD (Vol. 12, No. 4, 1990). *"This volume provides an excellent overview of fundraising with special application to libraries. . . . A useful book that is highly recommended for all libraries." (Library Journal)*

Library Material Costs and Access to Information, edited by Sul H. Lee (Vol. 12, No. 3, 1991). *"A cohesive treatment of the issue. Although the book's contributors possess a research library perspective, the data and the ideas presented are of interest and benefit to the entire profession, especially academic librarians." (Library Resources and Technical Services)*

Training Issues and Strategies in Libraries, edited by Paul M. Gherman, MALS, and Frances O. Painter, MLS, MBA (Vol. 12, No. 2, 1990). *"There are . . . useful chapters, all by different authors, each with a preliminary summary of the content–a device that saves much time in deciding whether to read the whole chapter or merely skim through it. Many of the chapters are essentially practical without too much emphasis on theory. This book is a good investment." (Library Association Record)*

Library Education and Employer Expectations, edited by E. Dale Cluff, PhD, MLS (Vol. 11, No. 3/4, 1990). *"Useful to library-school students and faculty interested in employment problems and employer perspectives. Librarians concerned with recruitment practices will also be interested." (Information Technology and Libraries)*

Managing Public Libraries in the 21st Century, edited by Pat Woodrum, MLS (Vol. 11, No. 1/2, 1989). *"A broad-based collection of topics that explores the management problems and possibilities public libraries will be facing in the 21st century." (Robert Swisher, PhD, Director, School of Library and Information Studies, University of Oklahoma)*

Human Resources Management in Libraries, edited by Gisela M. Webb, MLS, MPA (Vol. 10, No. 4, 1989). *"Thought provoking and enjoyable reading. . . . Provides valuable insights for the effective information manager." (Special Libraries)*

Creativity, Innovation, and Entrepreneurship in Libraries, edited by Donald E. Riggs, EdD, MLS (Vol. 10, No. 2/3, 1989). *"The volume is well worth reading as a whole. . . . There is very little repetition, and it should stimulate thought." (Australian Library Review)*

The Impact of Rising Costs of Serials and Monographs on Library Services and Programs, edited by Sul H. Lee (Vol. 10, No. 1, 1989). *". . . Sul Lee hit a winner here." (Serials Review)*

Computing, Electronic Publishing, and Information Technology: Their Impact on Academic Libraries, edited by Robin N. Downes (Vol. 9, No. 4, 1989). *"For a relatively short and easily digestible discussion of these issues, this book can be recommended, not only to those in academic libraries, but also to those in similar types of library or information unit, and to academics and educators in the field." (Journal of Documentation)*

Library Management and Technical Services: The Changing Role of Technical Services in Library Organizations, edited by Jennifer Cargill, MSLS, MSed (Vol. 9, No. 1, 1988). *"As a practical and instructive guide to issues such as automation, personnel matters, education, management techniques and liaison with other services, senior library managers with a sincere interest in evaluating the role of their technical services should find this a timely publication." (Library Association Record)*

Management Issues in the Networking Environment, edited by Edward R. Johnson, PhD (Vol. 8, No. 3/4, 1989). *"Particularly useful for librarians/information specialists contemplating establishing a local network." (Australian Library Review)*

Acquisitions, Budgets, and Material Costs: Issues and Approaches, edited by Sul H. Lee (Supp. #2, 1988). *"The advice of these library practitioners is sensible and their insights illuminating for librarians in academic libraries." (American Reference Books Annual)*

Pricing and Costs of Monographs and Serials: National and International Issues, edited by Sul H. Lee (Supp. #1, 1987). *"Eminently readable. There is a good balance of chapters on serials and monographs and the perspective of suppliers, publishers, and library practitioners are presented. A book well worth reading." (Australasian College Libraries)*

Legal Issues for Library and Information Managers, edited by William Z. Nasri, JD, PhD (Vol. 7, No. 4, 1987). *"Useful to any librarian looking for protection or wondering where responsibilities end and liabilities begin. Recommended." (Academic Library Book Review)*

Archives and Library Administration: Divergent Traditions and Common Concerns, edited by Lawrence J. McCrank, PhD, MLS (Vol. 7, No. 2/3, 1986). *"A forward-looking view of archives and libraries.... Recommend[ed] to students, teachers, and practitioners alike of archival and library science. It is readable, thought-provoking, and provides a summary of the major areas of divergence and convergence." (Association of Canadian Map Libraries and Archives)*

Excellence in Library Management, edited by Charlotte Georgi, MLS, and Robert Bellanti, MLS, MBA (Vol. 6, No. 3, 1985). *"Most beneficial for library administrators . . . for anyone interested in either library/information science or management." (Special Libraries)*

Marketing and the Library, edited by Gary T. Ford (Vol. 4, No. 4, 1984). *Discover the latest methods for more effective information dissemination and learn to develop successful programs for specific target areas.*

Finance Planning for Libraries, edited by Murray S. Martin (Vol. 3, No. 3/4, 1983). *Stresses the need for libraries to weed out expenditures which do not contribute to their basic role–the collection and organization of information–when planning where and when to spend money.*

Planning for Library Services: A Guide to Utilizing Planning Methods for Library Management, edited by Charles R. McClure, PhD (Vol. 2, No. 3/4, 1982). *"Should be read by anyone who is involved in planning processes of libraries–certainly by every administrator of a library or system." (American Reference Books Annual)*

For Product Safety Concerns and Information please contact our EU representative GPSR@taylorandfrancis.com Taylor & Francis Verlag GmbH, Kaufingerstraße 24, 80331 München, Germany